Beyond

Unleashing the Potential of
Women in Law

EDITED BY LAURA SLATER

Head of events and books
Leah Darbyshire

Commissioning editor
Laura Slater

Editorial assistant
Edward Bowes

Published by ARK Group:

UK, Europe and Asia office
6–14 Underwood Street
London, N1 7JQ
United Kingdom
Tel: +44(0) 207 566 5792
publishing@ark-group.com

North America office
4408 N. Rockwood Drive, Suite 150
Peoria IL 61614
United States
Tel: +1 (309) 495 2853
publishingna@ark-group.com

www.ark-group.com

Layout by Susie Bell, www.f-12.co.uk

Printed by Canon (UK) Ltd, Cockshot Hill, Reigate, RH2 8BF, United Kingdom

ISBN: 978-1-78358-288-4

A catalogue record for this book is available from the British Library

© 2017 ARK Group

Contents

Executive summary... vii

About the authors... xi

Chapter 1: Cheaper to keep 'er – The economic impact of losing
female talent at law firms..................................... 1
By Paola Cecchi-Dimeglio, behavioral economist and chair of
Harvard Law School's Executive Leadership Research Initiative
for Women and Minority Attorneys at the Center on the Legal
Profession

    The power of big data to quantify the loss....................2
    What's included in the cost of turnover?.....................3
    Women leaders: Expensive to replace 4
    The implications 7
    Conclusion...7

Chapter 2: Fix it, not them – How to increase the number of
women in positions of power................................... 9
By Patricia K. Gillette, keynote speaker and former law firm partner

    1. The Mansfield Rule...................................... 10
    2. Enhancing opportunities for building client relationships .. 11
    3. Scanning performance reviews and feedback for gender
    inequities 13
    4. Implicit bias training 13

Chapter 3: Getting rid of mindless barriers to advancement ... 17
By Ellen Ostrow, PhD, PCC, CMC, founding principal of Lawyers
Life Coach

    Psychological inflexibility 20
    Psychological flexibility 22

Acceptance and commitment training (ACT) to reduce
biased responding. 23
Research evidence. 25
ACT for women lawyers 27

Chapter 4: Balance – A radical new "B word" for the powerful
woman 33
*By Janice P. Brown, founder and senior partner in the Brown Law
Group*
What is power? 33
What does a powerful woman look like? 34
What is true power? 39
When do you become "powerful beyond measure?" 41

Chapter 5: Reclaiming the next generation – Understanding
and leveraging millennials in your workplace. 43
By Katherine M. Larkin-Wong, associate at Latham & Watkins LLP
What defines "millennial"? 44
Are millennial lawyers the same and what can law firms do
to keep them? 46
Millennials are here to stay – How will you engage them? 53

Chapter 6: Getting down to business development – What
works for women? 57
By Carol Frohlinger, Negotiating Women Inc.
What should women keep doing? 58
What should women do more of? 60
What should women do less of?. 62
Appendix A: Summary of "Business Development in the
'New Normal'" 64

Chapter 7: Striking the self-promotion balance – Demonstrating
your value without being the obnoxious one in the room 69
*By Debbie Epstein Henry, DEH Consulting, Speaking, Writing;
co-founder and managing director of Bliss Lawyers*
1. Be great 70
2. Be prepared 70
3. Observe others. 71
4. Credit others 71

5. Benefit others. 71
6. Get help 72
7. Own it 72
8. Take risks 72
9. Make the ask 73
10. Show initiative 73
11. Pay attention to the details. 73
12. Understand you will mess up 74
13. Develop a signature. 74

Chapter 8: Does size really matter? 77
By Cathy Fleming, partner at Fleming.Ruvoldt PLLC
Mistake #1: Always believing what Big Law managers
tell you 80
Mistake #2: Not marketing on a daily basis 80
Mistake #3: Targeting the wrong clients 81
Mistake #4: Not making sure you are happy 81
Mistake #5: Thinking Big Law is the only source of excellent
lawyers 81
Mistake #6: Believing that clients will come to you just
because you are a good lawyer 82
Mistake #7: Not respecting adequately the referring source
of business 82
Conclusion 83

Chapter 9: Using personal interests to help make it rain 85
By Audra A. Dial, managing partner, Atlanta office of Kilpatrick
Townsend & Stockton
Social outings 85
Vision boarding 86
Book club 87
Gift giving 88
Celebrating anniversaries of success 88
Monster jam 89
Holiday lights at the Botanical Garden 89
Final thoughts. 90

Executive summary

The lack of women in power positions represents a poor return on investment for law firms, and could be costing them far more than they think in both economic and cultural terms. Quite aside from the widely accepted understanding that more diverse teams perform better, research shows that it actually costs more and takes longer to replace female partners than their male colleagues.[1] Moreover, the scarcity of women mentors could be having a long-lasting effect on up-and-coming female associates.

The problem is far from new but law firms' usual answers – business development training, diversity programs, investment in "women's initiatives" – doesn't seem to be having much of an effect, despite the collective millions firms are spending on these. The numbers of women attaining power positions in law firms have remained static for decades. By contrast, the percentage of women holding GC positions in Fortune 500 companies is growing, and women are increasingly likely to be found in in-house roles.

Packed with fascinating insight, experience, and research from a broad range of lawyers, coaches, academics, thought leaders, and consultants, *Beyond Bias: Unleashing the Potential of Women in Law* considers just how much firms are costing themselves by failing to promote and retain talented women, the reasons their efforts have so far seen so little return, and the practical steps they can take to start to move the needle. We'll also consider what women can do more of to create and seize opportunities, claim credit where it's due, and get the most out of their business development efforts, wherever they practice.

In the opening chapter, based on her extensive research Paola Cecchi-Dimeglio, behavioral economist and chair of

Harvard Law School's Executive Leadership Research Initiative for Women and Minority Attorneys at the Center on the Legal Profession, examines and enables the quantification of the monetary impact of losing and replacing female talent, and she outlines what firms should be doing to identify and mitigate turnover risk.

Following on from this, Patricia K. Gillette, a former law firm partner and now a sought-after keynote speaker and author, looks at what law firms are currently doing to hold on to their female stars – and why it's just not working. She suggests several ideas that law firms could consider to open up much needed opportunities for women to maximize the training they are receiving, and to move into positions of power and leadership.

Opportunity is a key word when it comes to career progression. The best business development training cannot help someone to seize an opportunity that never arises. Ellen Ostrow PhD, founding principal of Lawyers Life Coach, explains in the next chapter how implicit biases and psychological inflexibility can prevent women from being offered opportunities to progress – and, equally, how these may be preventing women from seeking or accepting those same opportunities. She describes acceptance and commitment training (ACT) as a proven and powerful tool in recognizing and overcoming these internal barriers to advancing women in the law.

This is followed by a chapter from Janice P. Brown, founder and senior partner in the Brown Law Group, who explores what it really means to be powerful, rather than simply to wear the trappings of power. She explains how inner power – built on a commitment to authenticity – can benefit women in the legal profession from both a personal and professional point of view.

To consider women in isolation from the rest of their generation is to miss part of the puzzle; the issues that were key for baby boomers are not necessarily those that motivate or frustrate a millennial. Katherine Larkin-Wong, an associate at Latham & Watkins LLP and a "proud millennial", encourages firms to think of their up-and-coming female stars in the context of their generation (now the largest section of the workforce). In the next chapter, she considers what firms should be doing to ensure they understand the motivations and preferences of their millennial lawyers in order to help them to develop.

Carol Frohlinger, founder of Negotiating Women Inc., then shares research into men and women's preferences in terms of their business development styles, and she explains how the results can help women to understand the best activities to focus on in order to progress in their careers.

One of the business development techniques that many people struggle with is self-promotion – and this is especially true of women. While women are more inclined to downplay their successes, when they do claim due credit they often attract criticism and labels that would almost certainly not be leveled at a male colleague. Deborah Epstein Henry Esq, founder and president of Flex-Time Lawyers LLC and co-founder and managing director of Bliss Lawyers, provides essential advice on how women can get self-promotion right – and use it to their advantage.

The final two chapters of this book share personal perspectives on forging successful careers in the law:

Cathy Fleming, a partner at Fleming.Ruvoldt who has run the gamut from Big Law to boutique firm, explains some of the mistakes and misconceptions that in her experience lawyers often make when they set out to build a book of business, and she shares essential business development lessons that apply regardless of the career route you take.

This is followed by a chapter from Audra Dial, managing partner of the Atlanta office of Kilpatrick Townsend & Stockton LLP, who explains how she has built a successful career on being authentic and playing to her own strengths and interests – and you can too.

Reference
1. Based on research undertaken by Paola Cecchi-Dimeglio. See Chapter 1 of this book ("Cheaper to Keep 'er – The economic impact of losing female talent at law firms") for more on this topic.

About the authors

Janice P. Brown is the founder and senior partner in the Brown Law Group. Growing up in Montana, Janice went to work for the US Justice Department as a trial attorney in the tax division in 1984. In 1987, she was chosen as Trial Lawyer of the Year at the US Department of Justice. This early recognition would prove to be one of many honors and awards to follow. Janice went on to be a partner in the firm Seltzer, Caplan, Wilkins and McMahon. She also began to visualize the client-focused philosophy that would be the basis for her own firm.

Janice has been a mentor to numerous young lawyers, most significantly in her role as a former TIPS Council member. Over the past seven years, she has routinely spoken on attorney career and business development issues for the ABA and other professional legal organizations. In addition, she has developed programs within her own law firm that she later tested and taught to others in external law firm environments. Janice has provable results. As a result, she decided to launch Beyond Law, a consulting business focused on helping other lawyers reach their full potential; developmentally, professionally, and financially.

As a part of Beyond Law, Janice teaches a simple-to-use business development tool named Cloudburst®. She has been using the Cloudburst® system for her firm since 2004. Consequently, every year since then, Janice's book of business, consisting of Fortune 1000 corporations, governmental entities, and local iconic businesses has grown to a multi-million-dollar book of business.

Janice attributes her success in part to adapting proven business principles to the practice of law. Those principles include setting goals, examining beliefs, applying emotional intelligence and time management. As a practicing attorney, Janice is uniquely qualified to assist lawyers in transforming their practices without compromising their authenticity or their lives and by creating more independence, flexibility, and financial reward.

Paola Cecchi-Dimeglio, JD, LLM, PhD, is a behavioral economist and chair of the Executive Leadership Research Initiative for Women and Minority Attorneys at the Center for the Legal Profession at Harvard Law School and a Senior Research Fellow, jointly appointed at HLS and Harvard Kennedy (WAPPP). She can be reached at pcecchidimeglio@law.harvard.edu.

Audra A. Dial is the managing partner for Kilpatrick Townsend & Stockton LLP's Atlanta office. Audra is an experienced litigator practicing in the firm's nationally recognized Patent Litigation Team, in addition to handling complex commercial litigation involving technology. She focuses her practice on complex federal court litigation involving trade secrets, patent disputes, restrictive employment covenants, and complex business disputes involving intellectual property. Audra has obtained favorable verdicts in many high-profile intellectual property disputes, including on behalf of several Fortune 500 companies. She has represented companies whose intellectual property was misused both domestically and abroad.

Audra was recognized by Children's Healthcare of Atlanta as one of 2016's Women of Substance and Style and by the *Atlanta Business Chronicle* as a Woman Who Means Business in 2015. She received the Tapestri 2015 Legal Team of the Year award for her pro bono efforts on behalf of a victim of human trafficking. In 2014, Audra was recognized by Pathbuilders with the Inspiria Award and by the *Daily Report* in its 2014 Verdicts Hall of Fame for intellectual property litigation. Audra was honored by the State Bar of Georgia and the Georgia Supreme Court Chief Justice's Commission on Professionalism in 2013 with a Justice Robert Benham Community Service Award for her significant contributions to her community beyond her legal work. She is a member of the Leadership Atlanta class of 2016 and the Leadership Georgia class of 2014. Audra has also been recognized as a 2011 POW! Award winner by Women*etics*, a 2011 IMPACT Leader by *Business to Business* magazine, 2010 "Up and Comer" by the *Atlanta Business Chronicle*, Junior League Woman to Watch, a Georgia "Super Lawyer" from 2013–2015, and was recognized as one of the top 50 women attorneys in Georgia in 2016. Audra has been profiled by *Chambers and Partners* in its Women in Law section.

Audra earned her J.D. from William and Mary School of Law. She is involved with the Trade Secrets Committee of the Intellectual Property Owners Association, Women in Electronic Discovery, and the National Association of Women Lawyers. Audra received her Bachelor of Arts from American University, where she graduated cum laude in Interdisciplinary Studies.

Cathy Fleming is a refugee from Big Law and a name partner in a nine-lawyer firm with offices in New York City and the Meadowlands, New Jersey. Previously she served as chair of a White Collar Group, Chair of Tax Investigations Group, and as managing partner of a New York City Office of several AmLaw 200 firms. Cathy is a former federal prosecutor, including serving as chief of special prosecutions as an assistant united states attorney in the District of New Jersey.

Cathy focuses her practice on complex civil litigation and white-collar criminal cases. She has extensive experience in commercial, securities, employment, tax, antitrust, health care law, and international extraditions. Cathy has tried more than 60 cases to verdict, most of which have been in federal courts, including in New York, New Jersey, Florida, Texas, Massachusetts, Pennsylvania, Illinois, and California. She conducts internal integrity audits and investigations for corporations and public bodies. She also provides counsel to corporate management and committees and has represented members of special committees in defense against shareholder complaints in federal and state tender offer litigation.

Cathy represents companies and their executives and employees in criminal, tax, SEC, and other federal and state investigations. A significant portion of Cathy's work cannot be disclosed, since the matters were never made public.

Cathy is a past president of the National Association of Women Lawyers. She has been named a Super Lawyer in New York each year since its inception in 2006. Cathy has been married to Steven John Abrams since 1980. They have two grown children and a very spoiled Cavalier King Charles spaniel.

Carol Frohlinger is the president of Negotiating Women Inc., an advisory firm committed to helping organizations to advance talented women into leadership positions. Co-author of *Her Place at the Table: A Woman's Guide to Negotiating Five Key Challenges to Leadership Success*, Carol has over 15 years' experience in designing, developing, and delivering highly customized programs for executive women.

Using social science research about the systemic factors that impact female leaders as the context, Carol's approach emphasizes practical skills that equip women to position themselves to best advantage. Among the topics she focuses on are leadership, communication, personal branding, strategic networking, and of course negotiation. Her current research is focused on the systemic issues that women in professional services firms must negotiate to succeed, particularly those related to business development. Her recent white paper, "Business Development in the 'New Normal'", was published by Thomson Reuters Legal Executive Institute and included recommendations for actions professional services firms can take to improve results for both men and women.

On the organizational change side of the gender parity challenge, Carol consults with senior leaders, designs diagnostic surveys, conducts focus groups with women at all levels, and advises firms about how to launch and support women's initiatives that deliver a solid return on investment.

Carol recently served as an advisor to a team comprising six law firm partners that won third place in the Women in Law Hackathon (a "shark tank" style competition) intended to create innovative solutions to the gender equity problem in the legal profession. She is also the "practitioner in residence" at the Women, Leadership and Equality Program at the University of Maryland Francis King Carey School of Law. Carol is an affiliated faculty member of the Simmons School of Management and teaches at the Kenan-Flagler Business School at the University of North Carolina at Chapel Hill. Formerly, Carol served on the faculty of the University of California, Hastings College of the Law Leadership Academy for Women. Her advice has been featured by *The Today Show*, *CBS MoneyWatch*, *NPR*, and the *New York Times*, among other mainstream media. Frequently called upon to provide expert input by publications serving professional services firms, Carol also contributes articles to specialty journals such as the ALM Law Journal's *Marketing the Law Firm*.

Carol serves on the Women in the Legal Profession Committee of the New York City Bar Association and formerly co-chaired its Business and Leadership sub-committee. She co-authored "What You Need to Know About Negotiating Compensation", a publication of the American Bar Association's Presidential Task Force on Gender Equity and also served on the New York State Bar Association's Task Force on the Future of the Legal Profession. Carol volunteers with The Thirty Percent Coalition, an organization with a mission to increase the number of women on the boards of America's publicly held companies. She has been honored by The International Alliance for Women with its "World of Difference Award" and was named to the Top 50 Most Influential Women List by the *Irish Voice*.

Carol holds a J.D. from Fordham University School of Law.

Patricia K. Gillette is one of the country's leading experts and most sought-after speakers on gender diversity and equality. She was a top-rated employment lawyer and litigator for 40 years as well as a major rainmaker in her firms. In 2015 she resigned as a law firm partner to pursue her passion for changing the legal profession as an author and keynote speaker. Patricia was also invited to join JAMS and now spends some of her time mediating employment-related cases.

In her writings and presentations, Patricia focuses on how to succeed in the high-powered, fast-paced business environment of today. Relying on research studies she commissioned, as well as her own experiences and charismatic style, Patricia is able to inspire audiences to think positively and practically about how they can realize their personal and business goals. She also brings thought-provoking ideas on how to bring meaningful change to law firm and corporate structures to increase diversity and inclusion.

In recognition of her work to advance women in the profession, she has received several awards, including the ABA Golden Hammer Award, the California Women Lawyers Association's Fay Stender Award, the Transformational Leadership Award as one of the Top Women Rainmakers, and the Barristers Association of San Francisco Award of Merit.

Patricia is the co-founder of the 2006 Opt-In Project, the first nationwide initiative to refocus the discussion from work-life balance to the structural issues that impact the retention and advancement of women in the workplace. She has been a commissioner on the ABA Commission on Women in the Profession, the ABA's Gender Equity Task Force, co-chair of the BASF No Glass Ceiling Initiative, and she serves on non-profit boards, including Direct Women, which is dedicated to placing women attorneys on boards of public companies.

Patricia is the proud mother of two successful and enlightened sons and lives in Kensington, California with her husband of 42 years. She is an elected official of her town and active in community organizations and activities. For more information visit Patricia's website at www.patriciagillette.com.

Debbie Epstein Henry is an internationally recognized expert, consultant, and public speaker on women, careers, workplaces, and the legal profession. For nearly 20 years, hundreds of news outlets have featured Debbie's work including the *New York Times*, *NBC Nightly News*, and the *Wall Street Journal*. She is the author of two American Bar Association best-selling books, *Law & Reorder* (author, 2010) and *Finding Bliss* (co-author, 2015).

Debbie is a serial innovator. After practicing as a litigator, in 1999, Debbie founded Flex-Time Lawyers LLC (www.flex-timelawyers.com) to provide consulting, training, and speaking services. In 2006, she conceived of the Best Law Firms for Women initiative, a survey she subsequently ran for a decade with Working Mother to annually select the top 50 US law firms for women and report on industry trends. By 2008, Debbie's public speaking, press exposure, and advocacy enabled her to build a network of over 10,000 US lawyers. From there, she co-founded, with two colleagues, a second company, Bliss Lawyers (www.blisslawyers.com), that employs high caliber lawyers to work on "secondments" where the lawyers work on temporary engagements for in-house and law firm clients. Bliss has expanded to also handle temp-to-perm and direct hire placements and the company has lawyers employed for clients from New York to California.

Debbie has received numerous awards including, in 2017, she will receive the Anne X. Alpern Award, presented annually to a female lawyer who demonstrates excellence in the legal profession and who makes a significant professional impact on women in the law.

Katherine Larkin-Wong is a Litigation and Trial Associate in the San Francisco office of Latham & Watkins LLP and a member of the firm's Antitrust and White Collar practice groups. Katie is a former president and now board emeritus of Ms. JD, chair of the Social Impact Incubator, and a board member and chair of women's recruitment of the Associates Committee. She is a frequent writer and speaker on millennial lawyers and diversity in the law, and is herself a proud millennial. You can connect with her via Twitter @kmlarkinwong.

Ellen Ostrow, PhD, PCC, CMC is a strategic talent advisor, psychologist, certified coach, and founding principal of Lawyers Life Coach LLC. Since starting her firm in 1998 she has provided executive, leadership, and career coaching to many hundreds of attorneys at all levels of seniority in private practice, corporate legal departments, government, the judiciary, and non-profits. She also consults with practice groups, law firms, and corporate legal departments on strategic talent management and diversity and inclusion. Ellen is particularly known for her expertise on addressing barriers to the advancement of women in the profession and has spoken and written widely on these issues. She is the exclusive WILEF (Women in Law Empowerment Forum) endorsed leadership coach and serves as co-vice-chair of WILEF DC as well as on WILEF's global board. She is the co-chair of the board of the ThirdPath Institute and serves on the District of Columbia Bar's Board of Governors. Ellen is an advisor and coach for the DiversityLab's OnRamp Fellowship and a consultant for its Women-in-Law Hackathon. Ellen's deep understanding of the complexities of human behavior, motivation, emotion, and learning, derived from both her training in psychology and 30-plus years of experience working with individuals and organizations to facilitate change, combined with almost 20 years of working exclusively with attorneys and their employers, provides Ellen with a unique skill set among lawyer coaches and consultants. Ellen received her Ph.D. in Psychology from the University of Rochester and her coach training from MentorCoach©. She has served on the psychology faculties of three universities as well as teaching several master classes for MentorCoach©.

Chapter 1:
Cheaper to keep 'er – The economic impact of losing female talent at law firms

By Paola Cecchi-Dimeglio, behavioral economist and chair of Harvard Law School's Executive Leadership Research Initiative for Women and Minority Attorneys at the Center on the Legal Profession

We know there are separate barriers for recruiting and for sustaining female talent. When firms excel at acquiring female talent but do not follow up with excellence in sustaining that talent, relationships break down and talent is lost. In fact, diversity costs dearly when it's done wrong – when there's little effort to retain or promote female talent, and women walk out the door. That's because, in a profession where leadership is largely dominated by men, women leaders are rare. One of the ways I've gotten elite firms to focus on ways to foster a sustainable, attractive, gender-balanced culture is by drawing attention to the cost of losing top female talent.

Once law firms appreciate fully (and numerically) the real measure of funds lost in the departure of (female) talent, two options become blatantly obvious: get out of the diversity game in order to avoid throwing away money, or invest those inevitable losses in fostering a sustainable, attractive, gender-balanced culture.

Needless to say, there is no real dichotomy or dilemma here; abandoning diversity is not an option. Gender diversity is not merely ornamental, a gesture of corporate benevolence. Creating and maintaining a gender-balanced workforce is essential to business strategy, viability, and competitiveness. In fact, most conversations around diversity and female leadership focus on the business benefits. Firm leaders are beginning to understand that, when done right, diversity pays. Law firms with significant numbers of women leaders have a far better chance of solving complex problems; it leads to increased innovation, and it drives financial growth.

This article examines and enables quantification of the monetary impact of losing and replacing female talent. I've collected and analyzed years of data involving lateral movement at numerous US and international firms. The effort has been part of my research in nudging law firms to attract, retain, and promote women leaders.

The power of big data to quantify the loss

Arriving at an accurate cost of replacing employees is key, and assessing that cost with an understanding of the impact of gender difference is even more pertinent. To conduct this research, I mined cost and quality data of several domestic and international law firms over a period of ten years. One of the initial steps in nudging the organization to attract, recruit, promote, and sustain more women in leadership was, in fact, incentivized by drawing attention to the monetary cost of lawyer turnover, including direct and indirect cost, and the operational cost of replacing a highly productive lawyer (one who's reached their steady state with regards to performance). All of these elements were analyzed through a gender lens. The enormous data set yielded findings of very high statistical validity. They revealed a number of patterns about the cost of turnover. To my knowledge, it was the first study in the legal profession to look at turnover in this manner and demonstrate that it costs significantly more to replace female talent.

Analyzing the cost of replacing talent can be complex, but mathematical modeling based on big data facilitates analysis and enables predictive modeling. The equations may be elusive, but numbers identify patterns, improve approaches, and provide tools for tackling problems. In a nutshell, done right, diversity pays; done wrong, diversity costs.

Analysis of the data provides a wealth of information, confirms or disproves our gut feelings, and allows for informed choices "debiasing" strategic decisions. With respect to the loss and replacement of female talent, the data-analytics ecosystem approaches offer ways to deal with the challenge of achieving scaled solutions to increase diversity and inclusion in a meaningful and efficient way. The cost variability varies as a function of the firm size. But, whatever the size, law firms collectively spend billions of dollars each year to attract, recruit, train, and develop lawyers over several years, only to lose them. If they took time to assess them, organizations might act to stem the tide of these losses.

What's included in the cost of turnover?

Lawyers leave Big Law firms for a variety of reasons and destinations. Some go to competitors; some go in-house; some enter the public sector; some decide to leave the profession; some choose smaller, boutique firms. Still others are let go, are laid off, or decide to leave the job market altogether. All of these examples represent turnover, but they don't all have the same organizational or gender implications. Although large law firms base their business model on attrition, all turnover is not equal. There is a distinction between the "wanted" and the "unwanted", the necessary and the unnecessary – between functional (beneficial) and dysfunctional (harmful) turnover.

Turnover is costly; it impedes overall business performance, and it may become increasingly difficult to manage. The vast majority of firms, including law firms, do not often quantify the cost of turnover. Actual calculations of lawyer turnover rates may vary, but no matter how the math is done, it is stunningly high.

What's included in the cost of turnover? Salaries, signing bonuses, relocation costs, recruiting costs, administrative time and revenue lost while the position is open, all figure into the calculation. Then there are the costs associated with onboarding, credentialing, and training. Last and more difficult to quantify are reduced productivity and decreased revenue while a new lawyer's practice gets up and running.

Let's say that the revenue lost as a result of the departure of one full-time attorney at a big firm is $5 million. (For superstar partners in prime practice areas, the figure can be closer to 10 times that amount.) Add to this loss the recruitment costs of 9–11 percent of the lawyer's compensation and startup costs (onboarding, credentialing, training, etc.) in the range of 22–24 percent of compensation. Using this revenue estimate, the total cost of losing and replacing the attorney ranges between $6,550,000 and $6,750,000.

In the halls of many firms, some whisper that the total cost of losing a lawyer can reach 1.5–2 times annual salary, especially for lawyers in a firm's most important practice groups. Moreover, talent lost from practice groups that are considered breadwinners – in particular, female talent – can be extremely damaging and more important that one might think. (Among other things, the group dynamic is badly shaken.)

Researchers studying turnover of other service providers offer additional information. A growing body of research links high turnover rates to shortfalls in organizational performance. The more extensive the social capital of the employee who left, the more dramatic the erosion of the firm's performance.

Other research demonstrates that employers can spend the equivalent of six to nine months of an employee's salary to find and train a replacement.

Finally, one study estimates that turnover-related costs represent more than 12 percent of pre-tax income for the average company and nearly 40 percent for companies at the 75th percentile for turnover rate.

Women leaders: Expensive to replace

You might think, given all the lateral moves in Big Law, that unceasing turnover is an unavoidable cost of doing business. After all, the business model of elite firms is built on attrition. The vast majority of firms don't even quantify the cost of turnover of their male and female talents.

Three findings are of particular interest:

- It costs more money to replace your stars than you probably think;

- To replace top female talent, it takes months longer and costs more (as a percentage of salary) than it does to woo top male talent; and

- Keeping star lawyers, especially female stars, satisfied at your firm should be a business priority, given the colossal cost of replacing them and the accompanying disruption to business performance. Yet, for too many firms, it's not.

A key finding of my research, one that impacts costs, is that it takes longer to replace female talent (see Figure 1). The time required for replacing a male lawyer ranges from six to 11 months. Replacing a female lawyer requires seven to 14 months. This finding has implications in terms of cost, revenue loss, and loss of performance within the organization.

Replacing female lawyers takes more time…

Firms take up to 14 months to replace top female partners, three months more than to replace their male counterparts.

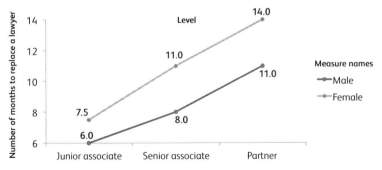

Figure 1: Replacing female lawyers takes more time…

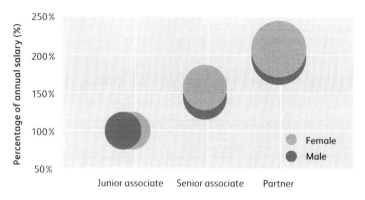

Figure 2: ...and female lawyers are more expensive to replace.

My research also indicates that the cost of replacing a female lawyer is higher than the cost of replacing a male counterpart (see Figure 2). The range varied based on the practice group the attorney belonged to, but the differential is about 10 percent for junior and senior associates and 20 percent for partners.

Specifically, concerning male lawyers, it costs 100–140 percent of salary to replace junior associates; 140–200 percent for senior associates; and 200–380 percent for partners. By contrast, the cost of replacing female lawyers is 100–150 percent of salary for junior associates; 150–210 percent for senior associates; and 210–400 percent for partners.

Here's another curious thing I've found. At many firms, the number of lateral partner hires made over the last 10 years exceeds the number of homegrown partners, especially for women. This need to move to become a partner is a considerable expense to the losing firms and in many cases suggests that firms are overlooking the talent under their own noses.

The departure of top female talent impacts firms in some ways that can be hard to see. It is often felt acutely by the teammates they leave behind. And their impact as role models in a profession with relatively few women at the very top cannot be underestimated.

The implications

Law firms must size up the turnover risk of specific lawyers, especially top talent. This proactive approach can assist law firms in several ways. First, thinking in terms of the turnover risk of specific employees should prompt an organization to invest time and resources into those employees who create the high levels of value but are significantly at risk for departure. In a nutshell, it allows firms to forecast an employee's potential decision to leave. Second, anticipating this potential loss, the firm can nudge the relationship or the environment to retain the employee, retain a talented workforce, and thus maintain a competitive advantage.

The broader implication is that firms must adjust their female talent strategies to grow and retain female leaders. One of the first steps is to understand the cost and reasons for female turnover at your firm.

Then you need to operate diversity efforts to benefit your firm and retain top women – not balloon the cost of doing business by attracting these stars, training them, and then watching them walk out the door.

These approaches won't prevent every star from making a move to another firm. And you'll likely need to continue to make some lateral hires, too. But my research suggests that firms can save themselves considerable cost if they take better care of the stars or would-be stars they already have.

Conclusion

Diversity is a reality and a necessity; it is here to stay. Businesses have to adapt to the new reality of an increasingly diverse workforce. They must also operate diversity in order to benefit the organization, not balloon the cost of doing business. A preferable response is to boost the firm's competitive advantage by prioritizing the retention of highly talented female attorneys. This strategy takes into account those drivers of turnover that can be nudged to create workplace dynamics that foster gender balance and retain more women.

Chapter 2:
Fix it, not them – How to increase the number of women in positions of power

By Patricia K. Gillette, keynote speaker and former law firm partner

Whatever we are doing in law firms to increase gender diversity in positions of economic and institutional power is not working. How do we know that? Simply look at the statistics. The number of women equity partners, in top rainmaking positions, at the top of the compensation schedules in law firms, and in lead positions for trials and deals has been stagnant for the last several decades.

And what are law firms doing about that? The same thing they have done for years – offering special training to women to account for the alleged skill deficiencies that keep them from moving up in their firms. The titles of the training programs may change from year to year and the trainers may change as well. But what doesn't change? The number of women in positions of power in their firms.

Why is that? Is it because women just can't be taught the skills they need to be successful power brokers? Is it because men are natural born leaders who can move into power positions with ease and successfully perform their responsibilities without the training that women supposedly need? Is it because women aren't really ambitious and don't want the power and financial rewards that come with leadership positions in their firms? These are some of the "explanations" that have traditionally been offered to account for the deficit in the numbers of women in positions of power in law firms, leading to the conclusion that if firms could just find a way to fix the women, all would be well.

Thus, law firms have been trying to "fix the women" for years – without success. And, unless one buys into the idea that women are not as able as men to assume positions of power, clearly something is wrong with the approach law firms have been taking to correct the lack of gender diversity in top leadership and power positions.

So what if we consider a new premise. What if we consider that it is not the women, but the system that needs to be fixed?

What we know about work assignments, client contact, lead counsel positions, compensation levels, and leadership positions is that these opportunities are, for the most part, controlled in most firms by white men. So that when those men are looking for attorneys to fill those positions, they consciously or unconsciously, look first towards people who look like them and maybe to the one or two women who have somehow gained some visibility in the firm. But most women are not on the radar screen for these positions.

In the past, firms have addressed this by giving women special "leadership" training or business development training. And while those are certainly valuable skills that are vital to the success of any attorney – regardless of gender – the effort to move women into positions of power cannot stop there. Why? Because training only works if it is coupled with opportunity. And it is the opportunity that has been lacking in the equation for firms trying to increase the number of women in positions of power.

How do firms change that? Below are several ideas that law firms could consider to ensure that women are able to maximize the training they are receiving and move into positions of power and leadership.

1. The Mansfield Rule

Arabella Mansfield was the first female lawyer admitted to practice in the United States. This rule is named after her because it too would be a first for the legal profession. The Mansfield Rule is modeled after the Rooney Rule that was adopted by the National Football League to increase diversity in team managers. The

Rooney Rule requires that there be at least one diverse candidate in the candidate pool for any NFL team manager opening.

The Mansfield Rule takes the same approach, but applies the Rule to all of the positions in law firms where power is wielded: the chair position, executive committee membership, compensation committee membership, practice group leaders, office managing partners, pitch teams, lead trial counsel positions. The Rule requires that the candidate pool for each of these positions or committees committees be made up of 30 percent women and other minority groups (although firms can certainly consider a higher requirement). It does not require that a woman be selected for the position or committee, but they must at least be considered.[1]

Why does this work? Because it raises the visibility of qualified women in the firm who might not otherwise be noticed and prevents firms from falling into the trap of giving leadership jobs, where these do go to women, to the same one or two. And, perhaps more importantly, it leads firms to think seriously about succession planning. With a mandate to consider at least one woman for each of these positions and committees, the firm will likely start identifying and nurturing potential candidates for these positions and committees before the selection process begins. This type of organized and thoughtful approach to attorneys who will be eligible to assume leadership positions in the firm not only increases opportunities for women, but also forces the firm to be more intentional in its development of future leaders. And it allows women who have received leadership training to utilize that training by being given opportunities to move into a leadership position in the firm.

2. Enhancing opportunities for building client relationships

Business development training is necessary and useful for firms. But, again, if it is done in a vacuum or in an environment where women are excluded from client opportunities offered to male attorneys, its impact is minimal. So, in addition to business development training, firms should consider several other actions that build upon the training:

- **Succession planning for institutional clients** – To the extent a firm has institutional clients that are tied to baby boomer partners, it behooves the firm to think strategically about how it will manage that client relationship after the baby boomer partner leaves the firm. The selection of that successor should be intentional. And that provides an opportunity to force consideration of a woman for the successor position. Of course, the person has to be acceptable to the client, but by requiring partners to consider gender diversity in making the decision of who will be selected, it is highly likely that more women will be given opportunities to take on major clients of the firm – opportunities that without succession planning would likely not be offered to them.

- **Monitoring of pitches and lead counsel assignments** – Exposure to clients is a huge part of successful business development. Yet most firms do not monitor who is selected to participate in major pitches for new business or who will meet with potential new clients. Instead these decisions are left to the partner who is heading up the pitch or the meeting. The same is true for lead counsel assignments on major litigation and corporate matters. And these lead counsel positions can offer women opportunities to demonstrate their legal skills to clients, obtain recognition externally, and build their reputations within the legal community.

  If the firm begins to monitor these kinds of opportunities – accounting for the gender of the attorneys chosen to participate – it can determine if men are being selected more often than women and can then take steps to correct that situation. And if more women are given opportunities like these, they can put the business development training they receive into effect.

3. Scanning performance reviews and feedback for gender inequities

Language is a powerful tool in law firms. The way an attorney's skills are described and the way attorneys describe themselves can impact opportunities. All the training in the world cannot combat internal documents that detract from or do not adequately describe the potential of the attorney. There is no question that some words convey greater abilities than others, even though that might not be the intention of the writer. For example, saying that Sally's presentation showed a lot of poise and preparation is not the same as saying Bill had incredible presence and was clearly well prepared for his presentation. While it may seem subtle, the former statement is more reserved and more feminine than the latter and can lead the reader to think that Bill is a stronger and better advocate than Sally.

We also know that women tend to underreport and downplay their strengths when asked to describe their achievements. So women will often attribute a success to "the team" while men will state that they "led their team" to great success. Again, a subtle change, but clearly conveying a different message and leaving the reader with a different impression of the two attorneys; the woman who bills herself as part of the team seems less responsible for the result than the man who led the team.

To avoid this kind of unintended consequence, firms can use programs that scan memos for gender based language – thus leveling the playing field and conveying praise and criticism more evenhandedly. This may result in stronger statements by managers about the women attorneys who work with them and may keep women attorneys from downplaying their own achievements and skill sets.

4. Implicit bias training

Everyone has biases. And lawyers in law firms are no exception to this rule. Raising consciousness about these implicit biases that hide in the shadows of everyday decision making in firms is critical to moving more women into positions of power and leadership. Because even if women are ready to move into these positions, the implicit biases of the men in power may keep them from doing so. For example, a male partner may choose not to put a women just back from maternity leave as lead counsel on a case that requires a lot of travel, remembering how his wife was distressed at having to leave her newborn for business. The intent is not necessarily bad, but the outcome is a denied opportunity for a woman. Whereas that same opportunity would likely not be denied to a new father.

If we want to increase the number of women in leadership positions in our firms, we have to begin to recognize and address these kinds of implicit biases. While they cannot be eliminated, attorneys can be trained to recognize their biases and to check their colleagues if they exhibit bias.

The beauty of these systemic changes is that they are easy to implement. More importantly, the impact of most of these actions can be measured. Thus, firms can determine whether the actions they are taking are in fact making a difference and, if they are not, the firms can try something different.

This idea of measuring whether actions designed to increase the number of women in power positions actually work seems like an obvious concept – it has been used in business for years. But, it has not been the practice of most law firms. Instead, firms have simply checked the box for various gender diversity and retention actions they take and never looked back to see if they are having the desired impact on the numbers. And that has led to the conclusion that the women in our firms are somehow deficient – leading to more training and still no increase in the number of women in positions of power.

The answer to this vicious cycle is for firms to take a more holistic approach to the desired goal of increasing the number of women in leadership positions. History tells us that training alone is not the answer because training without systems that provide opportunities for the persons trained to use what they have learned, cannot move the dial. Providing such training may feel good and even bring recognition to the firms for their efforts, but it does not address the systemic issues that keep women from advancing in their firms.

Of course, for law firms it is easier to say they need to fix the women rather than fix the system. But as long as access to opportunities to move into power positions is denied, the numbers will remain the same. Change that access, open the opportunities, level the playing field, and give women an opportunity to use the training they have received. That is how firms get real bang for their buck. And that is how we finally move the dial.

Reference

1. At the time of publication, around 20 US law firms are now trialling the Mansfield Rule.

Chapter 3:
Getting rid of mindless barriers to advancement

By Ellen Ostrow, PhD, PCC, CMC, founding principal of Lawyers Life Coach

> *"Between the stimulus and the response there is a space and in that space lies our power and our freedom."*
>
> Victor Frankl

We all know the sad story: the legal profession's efforts to advance women have barely moved the needle. Despite the fact that women have been entering law schools and the profession at numbers roughly equal to those of men for the past 30 years, the growth rates of women equity partnerships remain stagnant at 18 percent in the largest US firms.[1] The situation for lawyers of color is even more dismal, comprising only 8 percent of equity partnerships in elite firms. Among this small percentage, even fewer are women.[2,3] Women lawyers are retained at lower rates and earn lower incomes than their male peers.[4]

Law firms' stated commitment to diversity has manifested itself in a variety of ways. Firms have diversity committees, women's initiatives, and affiliate networks. Roughly 80 percent of firms[5] provide diversity training for their attorneys, and many offer a variety of skill development programs for women and diverse attorneys. The latter are grounded in the unstated assumption that if women can be "fixed", i.e., if they can communicate and conduct business development more like men, they will be more likely to advance. Firms have also increasingly offered flexible schedules to accommodate the needs of mothers in an effort to boost gender diversity.

The failure of these efforts to produce significant change has led to the recent focus on stigma and implicit bias.[6] Scholars and diversity leaders have noted the stigmatizing effect of taking advantage of reduced-hours options.[7] Implicit or explicit assumptions about women's diminished commitment to their careers results in fewer skill-building work opportunities. Male attorneys hesitate to invest in women as they build their families due to their automatic assumption that their investment will be squandered. This creates a self-fulfilling prophecy. Women see their opportunities for advancement fade and look outside their firms for better career options. Increased awareness of the effects of stereotypes and implicit biases about women's competence on a range of decisions including performance evaluations and compensation have also led to the recent emphasis on training lawyers about unconscious biases.

Cognitive science[8] has shown us that only 10 percent of our cognitive activity is what we think of as our "mind". These intentional, controlled cognitive processes require considerable effort and can address only one thing at a time. The other 90 percent are automatic, non-conscious brain processes which occur in parallel to intentional conscious thought. These automatic processes include gut feelings, emotional reactions, and rapid social judgments. When we respond to people based on social categories, we are operating according to stereotypes; that is, automatic assumptions about the characteristics of members of that group and, when it comes to gender, implicit beliefs about how women and men "ought" to behave. We are particularly prone to making these kinds of automatic evaluations when stressed, rushed, or overly busy – the norm of life in large law firms.

"In-group bias" operates similarly. It is more comfortable for people to associate with others similar to themselves. We also tend to judge similar others more favorably than those from whom we differ. Overly busy senior lawyers do not have the time to mentor and/or sponsor the large numbers of junior attorneys recruited to a firm. They are naturally inclined to focus their limited time and attention on those whom they perceive to hold the greatest promise of success. As a result, white males are more likely to receive career-advancing opportunities such as mentoring, sponsorship, and inclusion in informal networks.

Implicit bias training aims to reduce the impact of in-group, gender, and other biases. The premise behind this training has been that if lawyers can become aware of how their biases influence decisions about offering stretch assignments, evaluating work products, including women on pitch teams, and determining compensation, they would make bias-free assumptions and these barriers to women's advancement would be reduced.

This author knows of no published study demonstrating the effectiveness of unconscious bias training in advancing women or minority attorneys. Time and again, as a consultant I hear the biases of male attorneys – *after* they have received implicit bias training. These biases are subtle and insidious because they are not in the actor's awareness. For example, I recently spoke with the chairman of an AmLaw 100 firm about a woman appointed to the firm's executive committee. He complained that he'd heard her advocate for reducing the discrepancy between one woman partner's compensation and that of a similarly situated male. To him, this one comment revealed her singular interest in advocating for women and lack of concern with the larger interests of the firm. This is classic gender bias: women's "mistakes" (although I would hardly consider her advocacy mistaken) are remembered while those of men are rationalized or forgotten. He responded with defensive irritation when I questioned his assumption and reminded him of the firm's recent unconscious bias training.

Similarly, an Asian American coaching client shared her dismay when a male colleague approached her after the firm's implicit bias training, complaining about the stupidity of the program (which had been conducted by one of the premier diversity experts in the legal industry) and calling her by the name of another Asian American woman in the firm.

It's not that such training is misguided. Indeed, the existence of stereotyping and bias in decisions related to hiring, performance evaluations, and promotions has been amply demonstrated.[9] However, simply making attorneys aware that such biases exist and encouraging them to be vigilant has not proven to be efficacious. Despite the best of intentions, too many attorneys remain stuck, mindlessly acting based upon inflexible beliefs and, as a result, progress in the advancement of women and diverse attorneys at their firms remains stagnant.

What has been lacking is the implementation of a technology that actually changes the relationship between biased thoughts – whether conscious or implicit – and behavior. Fortunately, behavioral psychologists have developed, tested, and refined such a technology. A combination of acceptance, mindfulness, and values-based intervention strategies have been shown to directly change the relationship between biased thinking and behavior.[10] Not only have such interventions proven to alter behavior typically driven by stereotype-based assumptions; the very same kinds of strategies can be taught to stigmatized individuals – women and diverse attorneys – to facilitate their taking actions which might otherwise be blocked by limiting beliefs and fears. The same process that allows you to evaluate that your car is broken and leads you to trade it in rather than get it repaired can also enable you to evaluate a woman as less competent or uncommitted and lead you to take only her male peer to a pitch or to evaluate yourself as inadequate with resulting rumination about your mistakes and avoidance of challenges. It's all the same process and psychologists have provided the science to produce needed change. In this science lies the promise for the elusive reduction in barriers to the advancement of women in the law.

Psychological inflexibility

Psychological inflexibility is a term derived from psychological science that refers to the tendency to act based on how one thinks or feels rather than what would be most effective or meaningful in the moment.[11]

The mind is a complex set of interactive cognitive processes all of which rely on language. We use language both publicly and privately. During the average day most of us speak around 16,000 words.[12] But our thoughts – our internal voices – produce thousands more. Everyone experiences this constant internal chatter. "I'll lose this client if I don't get back to him today"; "What was that associate thinking when she wrote that out-of-office message?"; "These young attorneys have no work ethic"; "Why don't women step up for positions of power?" are but a few examples.

Language is quite useful and effective for analyzing legal problems, sharing knowledge, developing rules for effectively guiding behavior, learning from the past, and planning for the future. However, we also use language to compare, evaluate, and criticize both ourselves and others, to make biased assumptions about the potential of people who are different from us, to judge others based upon their group membership, as well as to limit our own potential in response to actions that stem from these judgments.

When these thoughts, judgments, beliefs, and rules make us insensitive to important information in our environments or lead us to behave in ways that are ineffective or inconsistent with our most important values and goals, we are said to be "hooked" by them.[13] We lose sight of the fact that these are just thoughts and instead treat them as facts. The thought that a woman could not possibly have originated such a large matter is accepted as a truth and origination credit is assigned to her male colleague.

Our thoughts, feelings, and assumptions can dominate our actions and make us inflexible. Rigid cognitive rules about how others or we ourselves "should" behave make us insensitive to important contextual realities such as actual talent where we don't expect to see it. A psychologically inflexible response pattern might include acting on one's biased beliefs despite conflicting egalitarian values or avoiding interacting with stigmatized groups in order to avoid discomfort.[14] (For a recent example of this, consider Vice President Pence's confession to the *Washington Post* that he will never eat alone with a woman other than his wife.) Specific psychological skills are required in order to effectively cope with the automatic, implicitly biased reactions lawyers might have towards women and diverse attorneys. On a broad level, these are known by psychological scientists as psychological flexibility skills.

Psychological flexibility

Psychological flexibility is the capacity to experience thoughts, feelings, sensations, and memories as they are – not as what they say they are – and then act in a manner that is optimally effective within the present context and in the service of one's chosen values. So, for example, a white male attorney might notice his hesitancy to offer a woman attorney working a reduced-hours schedule the chance to meet an important client based on his not necessarily conscious assumption that she is more committed to family than career, and then recognize this impulse for what it is – an *assumption* rather than the *truth*. He may notice that his thoughts about lawyer-moms who have left the firm are bringing the past into the present, while the reality of the present situation is that this particular woman is here, now, in his office, requesting an opportunity to advance her career. He may then give her this chance because he values fairness and believes in the firm's commitment to diversity. When he offers her this opportunity he will do so despite the lingering thoughts and worries that naturally accompany his automatic assumptions. What is important to note here is that the thoughts and discomfort are not eliminated. Rather, he is no longer "hooked" by these internal experiences and is able to flexibly respond to the situation and his values.

Psychological flexibility is the capacity to be fully present and aware in the moment, to be open to and accepting of our experience, and, without changing that experience, to take action in the service of what matters most to us. Psychological flexibility puts the thinker rather than the thought in charge of choices and actions. It involves being sensitive to the subtleties of context to which rigid rules and biases make us blind. A psychologically flexible attorney accepts that all human beings have these undesirable thoughts and emotions and, instead of trying to prevent or avoid them, knows how to get "unhooked" from them when they occur. This process allows us to make intentional choices to shift away from the unhelpful chatter in our minds, and to focus on actions that are aligned with our most important values.

Psychological flexibility training combines acceptance, mindfulness, and values-based intervention strategies to enable individuals to flexibly respond, being mindfully aware of their biased reactions without acting on them, and instead to engage in what would be effective and meaningful in the moment, despite the discomfort that might arise. Such training would enable attorneys to courageously and compassionately face difficult thoughts and emotions, to hold them lightly, and then to take action to accomplish valued diversity and career goals.

Acceptance and commitment training (ACT) to reduce biased responding

Some consultants in the legal diversity community have advocated the use of mindfulness practices for reducing implicit bias.[15] Although mindful awareness is a critical component of ACT, it is only one component. ACT is a behavioral intervention designed to create more psychological flexibility by helping us come into greater contact with our experience while undermining the dominance of mindless thoughts and gut reactions. ACT includes training in:

- Present moment awareness;
- Acceptance of self and others;
- Meta-awareness of oneself as the perceiver who can hold many perspectives and think many thoughts;
- The capacity to "unhook" from unhelpful thoughts and emotions;

- Values clarification; and
- "Walking your talk", i.e. taking committed action that is aligned with values.

ACT does not work to change thoughts, feelings, or biases. Rather it accepts them as a natural part of the human condition, of the way our brains are wired and how embedded we are in an internal and external world of language. Instead it trains people to change their relationship to internal events, to stand back and notice them without judging them and without being driven by them. In this sense, it has the potential to be particularly attractive to lawyers taught to value their objectivity.

ACT diminishes the defensiveness so frequently elicited by diversity and implicit bias training. There is no moral value placed on biased internal experiences. They are simply normalized as a natural part of our language-based cognitive processes. Furthermore, any defensiveness that comes up is simply seen as another hook. Whether the thought is "I am not biased" or "I don't have time for this", each is treated as simply a thought and the thinker is taught to notice, without judgment or struggle, to accept the thought's presence, and to question the thought's "workability"; that is, the extent to which it is helpful in the particular context in which it occurs.

In encouraging people to accept the content of their thoughts as merely thoughts, and feelings as simply feelings, ACT discourages blame or shame for having these thoughts and emotions. There is nothing wrong with the individual. They are simply stuck thinking a thought that is capturing them and making it difficult to take more effective action. Rigid rules and self-defeating thoughts are treated with curiosity. Individuals learn to treat themselves with compassion rather than vilify themselves for having such politically incorrect beliefs. We are not in control of the heuristics we have learned and research repeatedly demonstrates that stereotypes are highly resistant to change. Trying not to think a thought generally makes it more likely that it will come to mind. Try not thinking about a white bear.[16] Fighting with or criticizing ourselves for having particular thoughts or feelings typically makes them more persistent. Imagine, for example, telling someone wired to a lie detector not to feel nervous.

While unconscious bias training typically teaches that stereotyping is a normal cognitive process in which we all engage, it does not provide concrete tools to enable attorneys to accept these "unacceptable" thoughts. While such training can be quite effective at helping lawyers understand what unconscious bias is and how it works, in general, it does not typically provide effective tools for identifying these thoughts within oneself when they occur. Nor does it include effective strategies for unhooking from these thoughts and taking effective action while uncomfortable thoughts and feelings continue to occur.

ACT encourages us to take action even while our minds may be telling us to do the opposite. It helps us do what will work despite our feelings of discomfort. *It is this focus on learning the skills for taking effective action in the face of such automatic thoughts and feelings that makes ACT so distinctive from previous efforts to reduce the unconscious biases that block the advancement of women in the law.*

Research evidence

While ACT has yet to be tested in the legal environment, there is a large body of evidence that it can produce improved performance, job satisfaction, and employee engagement in the workplace[17] as well as reduce stigmatizing attitudes and behaviors. In fact, psychological flexibility has been found to be a better predictor of workplace effectiveness than emotional intelligence.[18] The implications of this for law firm leadership are profound.

Mindfulness training, a central component of ACT, involves learning to purposefully pay attention to the present, including our internal chatter, emotions, and sensations in an open, accepting, non-judgmental manner. Ellen Langer[19] describes mindfulness as the process of drawing novel distinctions, and notes that doing so keeps us situated in the present, making us more aware of the context and perspective of our actions than if we rely upon categories and distinctions drawn in the past. When we do the latter, rules and habits are more likely to govern our behavior, making us blind to the details of the current context and resulting in mindless behavior. Simply stated, behavior triggered by unconscious bias is mindless behavior.

Research demonstrates that mindfulness reduces prejudiced responding of white participants judging black defendants[20] as well as sexist beliefs and benevolent sexism in men towards women violating traditional gender roles.[21] Teaching children to be more mindful of their thoughts about people with disabilities resulted in less biased behavior and avoidance of disabled persons, even though there was no attempt to censor or suppress stereotyped beliefs.[22] Most importantly, ACT has been shown to produce a reduction in bias that was significantly greater than that produced by more traditional training in cross-cultural competency and the nature and consequences of stereotyping.[23]

As noted by Stephen C. Hayes, one of the founders of ACT and a prolific psychological scientist, there is every reason to believe that interventions that have proven to be so highly successful in reducing suffering[24] and enhancing performance[25] would be equally effective in addressing bias.[26] When attorneys enter into a verbal world in which their anxiety about losing clients is too high to cope with or their fear of failing keeps them from risking a stretch assignment, they are engaging in cognitive processes that are not unlike those that create a world where women with children or those who work reduced-hours schedules cannot be committed to their careers, or assertive women are too aggressive, or Asian women too timid to be leaders. The content may differ – the processes do not. Teaching attorneys to step back from their automatic biases and urges, to observe them dispassionately and with curiosity, acceptance, and compassion, and to take committed – albeit uncomfortable – action to advance women (if they value fairness and diversity) may provide the tools thus far missing from efforts to break barriers created by gender bias.[27]

ACT for women lawyers

As stated repeatedly in this chapter, the same kinds of cognitive, language-based processes that produce mindless, biased, inflexible behavior on the part of those with the greatest power in law firms can also limit the effectiveness of women lawyers. As an executive coach for women attorneys, I routinely hear the automatic, self-limiting thoughts and fears of women aspiring to success in their legal workplaces and satisfaction in their lives:

- "I don't know enough to answer the client's question."
- "I can't be a good mother and a good lawyer."
- "If you want something done well you have to do it yourself."
- "I can't leave work at work. I worry all the time."
- "I didn't say anything at the meeting because I was afraid of sounding stupid."
- "If I'm assertive I'm a b----, if I hold back, I'm weak."
- "I got screwed on my comp but there's no point saying anything."
- "I can't believe I'm being taken to task on how hard I am on junior lawyers! Do you have any idea what I went through when I was growing up at this firm?"
- "I just got elected to the firm's management committee, but I still feel like a fraud."
- "What if I move firms and it turns out the grass just seemed greener?"

Perhaps the most important thing for women attorneys to realize is that everyone has this kind of negative, often painful and worry-producing chatter constantly intruding. It is simply the stuff of which our minds are made. Efforts to suppress, avoid, or change these thoughts are futile or can even make them more frequent, intense, and persistent. It's also very easy to wind up avoiding situations that tend to evoke unhelpful thoughts and uncomfortable feelings and in doing so, avoid taking the risks and accepting the challenges that lead to career success and advancement.

For example, one very successful 10-year partner at an AmLaw 100 firm hated asking for help because she believed it made her look weak. She had no difficulty delegating to associates. However, her compensation was disproportionately low for her book of business and compared to others in her practice group, and she avoided developing the leadership network needed to increase her leverage in negotiating fairer compensation because these kinds of activities elicited shaming thoughts of weakness.

Coaching women lawyers to become psychologically flexible involves facilitating mindful awareness of self-critical and judgmental thoughts, rigid rules and "shoulds", internalized stigma, and anxiety-producing "what ifs?" They learn to notice these thoughts and feelings with acceptance for what they are – just thoughts and feelings rather than facts or reliable indicators of danger. The simple recognition that having these thoughts makes us nothing more or less than human is often very liberating. Similarly, understanding that our brains are wired to predict the worst under situations of uncertainty reduces the potency of worst-case-scenario thinking and enables these women to take committed action towards their most valued goals, carrying their uncomfortable thoughts and feelings along for the ride.

One client, a regulatory lawyer with a multi-million-dollar book of business in the very male-dominated financial industry, was stricken with doubt when she ascended to the firm's management and compensation committees. "I know I'm here but I keep thinking I've fooled everyone and sooner or later I'll be found out." Now after several months of coaching, she proudly talks about how noticing her thoughts and accepting them and herself with compassion helps her to unhook from her doubts, to refocus her attention on the task at hand, and to embrace her leadership responsibilities and opportunities in a mindful, intentional, and courageous way. She goes out of her way to reach out to younger women at the firm who she thinks may be struggling. She shares her journey, hoping that in seeing her humanity they too might begin to increase their own psychological flexibility.

A particular study on the effects of mindfulness on freeing women leaders from gender role constraints is worth noting.[28] When women speakers performed mindfully by doing something novel rather than following a script, they were perceived by male businessmen to be more charismatic, genuine, and better leaders than those who mindlessly followed their script, regardless of whether the script was crafted to fit a male or female gender role. Thus, being mindfully authentic provides the potential for women leaders in law firms to be perceived as effective and interpersonally attractive rather than being limited by the stereotypical double bind.

A psychologically flexible woman lawyer will experience all of the same self-stigmatizing thoughts, fears of taking risks, and pulls to avoid challenges as her less flexible peers. Her mind will continue to provide rigid rules about how to manage up, down, and sideways. She will differ from her less mindful colleagues in how she relates to these uncomfortable internal experiences. She will be mindfully aware that if she allows these thoughts to control her actions, she will stay stuck. She will understand the futility of ruminating about the validity of these thoughts. Instead she will ask herself whether holding tightly on to these thoughts, obeying old rules or avoiding situations that elicit discomfort are working in the long run to help her to be in charge of her career and her life. She will make intentional choices to shift away from the unhelpful chatter in her mind and to focus on actions aligned with her most important values. She will focus on the present moment and notice and respond effectively to goal-related opportunities. She will connect to her deepest desires for her own success and for gender equality, and she will take the next courageous challenge to move her own career forward, to find ways to integrate work and other valued aspects of her life, and to take one step at a time to break down the barriers to her own and other women's advancement.

References

1. *A Current Glance at Women in the Law*, ABA Commission on Women in the Profession, January 2017.
2. *2016 Report on Diversity in U.S. Law Firms*. National Association for Law Placement, January 2017.
3. Rikleen, L. S. "Women lawyers continue to lag behind male colleagues", *Report of the 9th Annual NAWL National Survey of Retention and Promotion of Women in Law Firms*, 2015.
4. Jaffe, A., Chediak, G., Douglas, E., and Tudor, M. *Retaining and Advancing Women in Law Firms*, Stanford Law School, 2016.
5. Rikleen, L.S. *op.cit.* p.3.
6. Pearce, R. G., Wald, E., and Balakrishnen, S. S. "Difference blindness vs. bias awareness: Why law firms with the best of intentions have failed to create diverse partnerships", *Fordham Law Review*, 83 (5), 2015. (2407–2455)
7. Williams, J.C. "The politics of time in the legal profession" *University of St. Thomas Law Journal*, 4 (3), 2007. (379–404)
8. Kahneman, D. *Thinking Fast and Slow*, New York: Farrar, Straus & Giroux, 2011.
9. *Fair Measure: Toward Effective Attorney Evaluations*, American Bar Association, Commission on Women in the Profession, 2008.
10. Hayes, S. C., Stroshal, K.D., and Wilson, K. G. *Acceptance and Commitment Therapy: The Process and Practice of Mindful Change*. New York: The Guilford Press, 2016.
11. Levin, M. E., Luomo, J. B., Vilardaga, R., Lillis, J., Nobles, R., and Hayes, S. C., "Examining the role of psychological inflexibility, perspective taking, and empathic concern in generalized prejudice", *Journal of Applied Social Psychology, 46*, 2016. (180–191)
12. David, S. *Emotional Agility: Get Unstuck, Embrace Change and Thrive in Work and Life*, London: Penguin Life, 2016.
13. Harris, R. *ACT Made Simple*, Oakland: New Harbinger Publications, Inc., 2009.
14. Chen, V. "Mike Pence is a prude, and so are big-law partners", *American Lawyer*, 5 April 2017. Available at http://www.americanlawyer.com/

id=1202783077180/Mike-Pence-Is-a-Prude-and-So-Are-BigLaw-Partne
rs?mcode=1202617075486&curindex=0; Also see Ostrow, E. "Can't we
just do lunch? ", Attorney at Work, 3 January 2012. Available at https://
www.attorneyatwork.com/cant-we-just-do-lunch/.

15. Nalty, K. "Strategies for confronting unconscious bias", *The Colorado
Lawyer*, May 2016. Available at http://bit.ly/1Njkkf2.

16. Wegner, D. *White Bears and Other Unwanted Thoughts: Suppression,
Obsession and the Psychology of Mental Control*, New York: The Guilford
Press, 1994.

17. Flaxman, P. E., Bond, F.W., and Livheim, F. *The Mindful and Effective
Employee*, Oakland: New Harbinger Publications, Inc., 2013.

18. Donaldson-Feilder, E., and Bond, F. W. "Psychological acceptance and
emotional intelligence in relation to workplace well-being", *British
Journal of Guidance and Counselling, 34*, 2004. (1887–203)

19. Langer, E. J and Moldoveanu, M., "The construct of mindfulness",
Journal of Social Issues, 56 (1), 2000. (1–9)

20. Greenberg, J., Schimel, J., Martens, A., Solomon, S., and Pyszcznyski,
T. "Sympathy for the devil: Evidence that reminding Whites of their
mortality promotes for favorable reactions to White racists", *Motivation
and Emotion*, 25, 2001. (113–133)

21. Gervais, S. J. and Hoffman, L. "Just think about it, sexism, and prejudice
toward feminists", *Sex roles, 68*, 2013. (283-295)

22. Langer, E. J., Bashner, R. S., & Chanowitz, B. "Decreasing prejudice by
increasing discrimination", *Journal of Personality and Social Psychology,
49 (1)*, 1985. (113–120)

23. Lillis, J. and Hayes, S. C., "Applying acceptance, mindfulness and values
to the reduction of prejudice: a pilot study", *Behavior Modification, 31 (4)*,
2007. (389–411)

24. Hayes, S. C. et. al. 2016, *op. cit.*

25. Flaxman, P. E. et. al. 2013 *op. cit.*

26. Hayes, S.C., Niccolls, R., Masuda, A. and Rye, A. K. "Prejudice, terrorism
and behavior therapy", *Cognitive and Behavioral Practice, 2002, 9*, 2002.
(296–301)

27. Lillis, J. and Levin, M. "Acceptance and mindfulness for undermining
prejudice" in Masuda, A. (ed.) *Mindfulness and Acceptance in Multicultural
Competency*, Oakland: New Harbinger Press, Inc., 2014.

28. Kawakami, C., White, J. B. and Langer, E. J. "Mindful and masculine:
Freeing women leaders from the constraints of gender roles", *Journal of
Social Issues, 56 (1)*, 2000. (49–63).

Chapter 4:
Balance – A radical new "B word" for the powerful woman

By Janice P. Brown, founder and senior partner in the Brown Law Group

> *"Our deepest fear is not that we are inadequate. Our deepest fear is that we are powerful beyond measure."*
>
> Marianne Williamson, A Return To Love: Reflections on the Principles of "A Course in Miracles"

What is power?

When asked to define "power", women lawyers typically describe influence over others, or external factors such as wealth or fame. According to our common-sense understanding of the term, power is defined as what others perceive about you, as opposed to what you perceive or know about yourself. Given the imbalance between the sexes in the legal leadership and the persistent "-isms" that remain in law, it is no wonder that women are often confused about what power is, what power means, and how to achieve it.

Consider, for instance, the gender-based double standards by which we measure the strength and ability of our leaders. Would it be possible, for example, for a woman to occupy the most powerful position in the land if she possessed all of the typical trappings of power, including influence, wealth, a high-profile spouse, an elite education, and a competitive, solid record of achievement in several high-ranking positions? Or would that woman's drive for power come across as pathological and unattractive – perhaps even corrupt? Would a woman born into a life of extraordinary wealth, privilege, and fame be considered a strong and respectable leader if she publicly luxuriated in her opulent lifestyle; exercised little to no restraint with her words and actions; made disparaging remarks about the opposite sex and other groups of people; and rambled incoherently about serious policy issues? What might change if the leader exhibiting such brazen incompetence and self-entitlement happened to be a man of great fortune and celebrity? And would it be possible for this leader, regardless of gender, to be consumed by insatiable insecurity, paranoia, and resentment, despite having reached the pinnacles of power and privilege?

When power is conflated with superficial status symbols and influence over others, it often amounts to little more than a mirage – a boastful display of fear and fragility masquerading as confidence and strength. Moreover, it is almost impossible to perceive of a powerful woman as anything other than an oxymoron within this limiting and unstable paradigm. Though defining power in relational and repressive terms may be intellectually unsound and spiritually hollow, this framework endures because it supports systems of inequality that benefit a privileged few. More specifically, this model of power reinforces patriarchy as a sense-making system that upholds male dominance in every aspect of our culture. Male privilege, in other words, consciously and unconsciously shapes the ways in which we all make meaning of and move through the world. For example, our culture's persistent gendering of that which is "powerful", and therefore superior, as masculine on the one hand, and the blanket devaluing of that which is feminine on the other, presents a taxing set of psychological and practical challenges for ambitious women in any professional environment. These challenges are compounded by the current political climate, where discourses of gender equality are met with intensified hostility, as well as by other organizing principles of identity, such as race, age, and sexuality.

What does a powerful woman look like?

The hostile resistance and suspicion towards female leadership within American culture is, in fact, so pronounced, that the very concept of the powerful woman is considered, by some, to be a uniquely American construct. Our ideas about powerful women tend to sway dramatically between fear and fascination, and these thoughts and feelings are constantly being worked out across various landscapes. Popular culture flirts with celebrating – even normalizing – an increasingly diverse array of powerful women, but these mainstream representations almost always fall short of delivering on their promises. With rare exceptions, powerful female figures are typically pushed to the narrative fringes; defined primarily by their work inside the home or by their relationships with men and children; or subjected to various forms of punishment and humiliation as a direct consequence of their power. The privileging of white, male-driven narratives that glorify individual triumph over external adversity is so entrenched in mass culture, that when a film like *Hidden Figures* (2016) – a historical drama about three brilliant black women who, against all odds, become an indispensable force in NASA's efforts to win the space race in the early 1960s – comes along, it not only sweeps up awards and smashes box office records, it practically becomes a social movement in and of itself. This demand for diverse, positive images of powerful women has even carried over into less obvious forms of visual culture. For instance, when Facebook COO Sheryl Sandberg noticed the striking gender biases throughout various stock photography collections, she teamed up with Getty Images to commission the "Lean In Collection", an extensive library of images depicting girls and women in leadership roles, as well as men engaged in equal partnerships with women at work and at home.

While positive representations of powerful women are gradually becoming more accepted and commonplace within mainstream visual culture, the powerful woman remains a subversive figuration in other contexts, including law. As a consequence of their gender, women who aspire to leadership roles often feel compelled to downplay their authentic power by overemphasizing what they perceive to be their "softer", more feminine side, which for many professional women, means their maternal side. Nearly two decades into the 21st century, motherhood not only remains the most socially acceptable space for women to lay claim to power, it also remains the cornerstone for the enduring cultural fantasy of "having it all" – a cute shorthand for the monstrous cluster of expectations by which society measures a woman's power and worth. The internal sense of purpose and validation many women derive from motherhood plays out against a broad social pressure to meet increasingly unreasonable standards of self-sacrifice. This doctrine of maternal self-sacrifice, combined with the insufficient support most working mothers receive from the government, their employers, and their partners at home, places women at a marked disadvantage for acquiring power in other contexts – let alone at a rate and level on par with their male peers. Women in law, for instance, face pressure on the one hand to soften their power in the workplace, but on the other hand, they fear that focusing on family will demonstrate a lack of commitment to the demands of firm life – the late nights, the frequent travel, and the stressful nature of the work itself.

What's more, the overlapping credos of self-sacrifice and "work that is never done" extend beyond motherhood into a broader culture of "busy-ness", where chronic over-scheduling has become something of a status symbol. In subscribing to busy-ness, we signal to the outside world that we're worthwhile because our time is in high demand from others. Self-care is thus reduced to an occasional, frivolous indulgence at best; and a vain, shameful waste of time at worst. At the same time, we find ourselves immersed in a consumer culture that demands constant self-improvement. Women in particular are bombarded with messages that not only amplify their existing insecurities, but also invent new flaws and lacks to be alleviated through conspicuous consumption. The multi-billion dollar diet industry, for instance, has been extraordinarily successful in selling women on the idea that they should take up less physical space – just as they are making significant strides in the long, hard fight to claim more space in the workforce, higher education, politics, art, activism, and many other male-dominated arenas.

Ironically, it is often exceptionally bright, high-achieving women like attorneys who find themselves paralyzed by feelings of inadequacy and compulsive approval seeking. These ambitious women are more likely to self-identify with the manufactured fantasy of having it all, and may even insist on the possibility of having it all at once – only to discover that the legal profession is brutally unaccommodating to this already impossible set of expectations, which keeps women tethered to feelings of failure, disappointment, and self-loathing. Despite more recent efforts to address gender inequity, the legal profession still lacks an unmistakable image of a powerful woman, and there is no clear pipeline to power for women navigating this stubbornly male-dominated field.

According to the most recent report from the National Association for Law Placement, white men comprise nearly 73 percent of partners in general, and the representational gains made by women and minorities at the partnership level have been dismayingly slow. Women currently make up nearly 18 percent of equity partnerships and nearly 30 percent of non-equity partnerships, with minority women remaining the most significantly underrepresented group at the partnership level.[1] A recent survey from the legal search firm Major, Lindsey & Africa finds that female partners can also expect to earn 44 percent less than their male counterparts.[2] Even women who do occupy high-ranking, rainmaking positions within law still speak about their power in uncertain and uncomfortable terms. They perceive power as something fundamentally oppressive, something to resist or outsmart rather than something they possess or wield to their advantage. In fact, it is not uncommon for female lawyers to view power as a *disadvantage* within the profession.

This reluctance to embrace power stems in part from the fear that men dislike powerful women, and men happen to be the decision makers determining who is going to succeed within the Big Law environment. This presumed dislike is sometimes expressed through inflammatory "b words" such as "bossy" or "bitch", both of which have taken on alternative meanings in recent years. Sheryl Sandberg, for instance, has led the charge in reframing "bossy" as a desirable executive leadership trait, and it's become increasingly fashionable for women to wear "bitch" as a badge of pride – as Tina Fey declared on *Saturday Night Live* back in 2008: "Bitch is the new black!" Though these notorious "b words" are having a feminist moment, they're still capable of freezing women by tampering with their confidence and professional growth. Being labeled a bitch could very well kill a woman's career in the legal profession, while men are unlikely to suffer any professional blows for behaving like or being known as an "asshole" or a "jerk" – in fact, such labels might even help them succeed in an identical setting. In any case, men are basically free from the psychological burdens of fearing or reclaiming any labels whatsoever.

In this ongoing struggle to advance their careers while still maintaining likability in a male-dominated work environment, some female attorneys have opted to rebrand their power as "influence", and seek advantages in being underestimated by their male peers. The popular concept of "soft power", for instance, offers a relatively non-threatening approach for influencing others through unassuming means of persuasion and appeal, rather than coercion or explicit directives. These superficial adjustments and coping mechanisms, however, have little to offer in the way of reworking the system that produces such inequality and frustration in the first place. Whether it's being frozen by a "b word", or being burnt out by the suffocating pressure to have it all, a paradigm that defines power in external and relational terms ultimately leads to despair – regardless of how we soften our approach, regardless of how closely we measure up to other people's standards of likability. True power requires an earnest understanding that liking oneself is far more important than gaining approval from others.

What is true power?

During a recent campus visit to the Stanford Graduate School of Business, globally renowned business leader, philanthropist, and all-around Renaissance woman Oprah Winfrey attributed her success to not being afraid to honor herself, and to her ability to connect with other self-actualized leaders whose work is grounded in a centered place. When Winfrey, for example, was searching for a CEO to helm her television network, OWN, she asked her job candidates a seemingly unorthodox question: "What's your spiritual practice?" Although a few candidates misinterpreted the question as an invitation to disclose their religious beliefs, Winfrey explained that her intention was to assess whether or not the candidates were committed to nurturing themselves and cultivating a rich inner life.

In accordance with Winfrey's understanding of authentic empowerment, one could surmise that such a centered person would not only have the genuine self-confidence to lead with intention and authenticity, but could also build the resilience and grit necessary to overcome obstacles that present themselves in every aspect of our lives. Sheryl Sandberg explores this very topic in her latest book, *Option B: Facing Adversity, Building Resilience, and Finding Joy*, which she co-authored with Wharton professor, Adam Grant. In drawing from a broad range of stories showcasing the importance of resilience in family, community, and workplace settings, *Option B* emphasizes resilience as an invaluable skill set developed over time. Sandberg, for instance, opens up about her own experience grieving the unexpected death of her beloved husband and the father of her children in order to demonstrate how women and others can overcome even the most tragic setbacks through building up a reservoir of internal power.

What Winfrey and Sandberg share is the knowledge that true power is not something that can be achieved, purchased, or acquired outside of oneself. Instead, it is a practice that is honed through personal reflection, authenticity, and vulnerability – three concepts that are not typically associated with power. As an internal energy within oneself that is honed, harnessed, and projected outwardly, true power can never be taken away, compromised, or destroyed; one owns one's true power and bears sole responsibility for its development. Though it is equally available to everyone, true power is especially liberating for women because it shucks power from the patriarchy, from the male gaze, from connotations of physical strength, as well as from the ideological tyranny of having it all. A shift towards true power thus requires a radical reclaiming of yet another loaded "b word": balance. When defined in relation to our prevailing notion of power as something conferred externally, balance is often reduced to another tidy euphemism for the cruel and unattainable expectations of having it all. Within the context of true power, however, balance names the radical, fearless insistence on developing a centered and authentic self, and sustaining relentless optimism in the face of adversity.

Despite the endorsements of prominent, visionary leaders like Winfrey and Sandberg, this notion of power as consciousness may still come across as fanciful or downright absurd to overachieving, intellectual types like lawyers. Fortunately, for the most skeptical and cynical among us, there also happens to be a growing body of scientific research that supports the existence of internal power and its many benefits. For instance, the internal strengths associated with true power, including knowingness, assuredness, contentment, charisma, and authenticity are foregrounded in David R. Hawkins' landmark study, *Power vs. Force: The Hidden Determinants of Human Behavior*. In this book, Hawkins lays out a scientific case for the existence of measurable energy relating to a spectrum of emotional states and levels of consciousness. His findings suggest that there are higher levels of energy associated with higher states of consciousness and positive emotional states; there is, for instance, more energy in a state of bliss than sadness, more in courage than shame. This model of internal power is also supported by research on the part of the brain called the "default network", which responds to internalized knowledge rather than external stimuli. In serving as the neurological basis for the self, the default network provides a mechanism for understanding the processes of self-awareness and transcendence, whereby the brain detaches from the external environment. Research suggests that it is possible to enlarge this section of the brain through internal work, and enjoy heightened levels of confidence as a result.

Though the results of true power – knowingness, assuredness, contentment, charisma, and authenticity – are extremely beneficial for the practice and business development aspects of law, the commitment to honoring oneself is an especially crucial undertaking for women in the legal profession. We know that lawyer burnout among women is rampant, and that the anger, fear, and cynicism that can help build up a successful lawyer eventually take a negative (sometimes fatal) physical and mental toll. These feelings of burnout and frustration are compounded by the fact that many female attorneys lack the training, confidence, and support necessary to build a robust book of business and achieve rainmaker status. By turning inwards, we're able to detach more easily from things beyond our control, whether it's in the courtroom or the office, within the profession at large, or within our private lives. It's through this sublime process of letting go that we become more charismatic. In developing charisma, we improve the space around ourselves and attract the right people and the right things at the right time – effortlessly. When we honor the call to balance and take time to nurture our best selves, we become more focused, creative, and productive. We make better, more intentional decisions. We're able to build the kind of authentic personal relationships that lead to abundance in all its forms, including influence, economic prosperity, professional success, and love.

When do you become "powerful beyond measure?"

Accepting total responsibility for your own true power – for your own success and fulfillment in life – is at once exhilarating and intimidating, for there are no shortcuts or excuses when it comes to true power. In making the conscious choice to honor yourself, you get to define what your most authentically empowered self looks like, and how you will go about bringing that vision to life within your own unique circumstances. This lifelong, moment-to-moment commitment to building genuine confidence begins with finding a spiritual practice that speaks to your authentic self and anchors you in the present moment. Start by reading inspirational books, writing in a journal, spending time in nature, listening to guided meditations, practicing silence, or enjoying a type of music that takes you out of your head – out of the constant background noise of anxiety and self-doubt.

Though the benefits are not always easily quantifiable or immediately felt, and your chosen practice is bound to feel daunting at times, the more time and effort you devote to developing internal power, the more authentic, charismatic, and resilient you become. In daring to turn inwards, in daring to prioritize balance, and in daring to combat the toxic belief systems that hold your authentic self hostage to fear, your internal work will inevitably yield some kind of positive outcome – even if you're not quite ready to believe that you are, in fact, "powerful beyond measure".

References

1. "Representation of Women and Minorities Among Equity Partners Has Increased Only Slightly," *NALP Bulletin*, April 2017, http://www.nalp.org/0417research. See also, National Association for Law Placement Inc., 2016 Report on Diversity in U.S. Law Firms", January 2017. Available at: http://www.nalp.org/uploads/Membership/2016NALPReportonDiversityinUSLawFirms.pdf

2. Olson, E. "A 44% Pay Divide for Female and Male Lawyers, Survey Says", *New York Times*, 12 October 2016. Available at: https://www.nytimes.com/2016/10/13/business/dealbook/female-law-partners-earn-44-less-than-the-men-survey-shows.html

Chapter 5:
Reclaiming the next generation – Understanding and leveraging millennials in your workplace

By Katherine M. Larkin-Wong, associate at Latham & Watkins LLP

> *"Stop trying to figure out Millennials and just include them."*
>
> Ms. JD/Above the Law Millennial Study Participant

They are officially the majority of today's workforce.[1] They are alternately described as entitled, lazy, and the "trophy generation"; and as creative, driven, and philanthropic. Heralded as the "Title IX generation" (i.e. they grew up in schools where girls were expected to have equal opportunities to boys), the most diverse generation ever, and a generation where men are equally interested in family life, millennials promise to challenge many law firms' status quo. Many diversity professionals believe that millennials may transition "women's issues" into "employee issues", based on how they view the world. No matter what you think of them, millennials[2] are entering your firms and clients' organizations in droves, and all firms must grapple with managing, retaining, and pitching to them. The question is, how?

In this article I explore some defining millennial characteristics and why they can feel challenging to law firms. I will report on original survey research conducted by Grover Cleveland, Darien Fleming,[3] and I, in conjunction with Above the Law and Ms. JD, to determine what millennial lawyers want, and how they may be different from their generation at large. Finally, I will talk about some of the best practices coming out of the survey and anecdotal experience, both my own as a millennial and those of the many millennials that I have worked with through Ms. JD and other organizations.

At bottom, the question for law firms is not whether you have to work with millennials: you do. It is *why* you should want to work with them, *what* attitude you will take in doing so, and *how* you can make them a huge asset to your firm. I hope this article is a starting point for answering those questions.

What defines "millennial"?

"You Raised Us, Now Work With Us"[4]

While we may not agree on the characteristics that describe millennials, we can agree about some of the critical events and societal changes that influenced them. And, while generalizations are always dangerous, there is plenty of research suggesting millennials, like every generation before them, have some uniting characteristics. In this section, I explore some of the research documenting the characteristics of the millennial generation at large. Later, I will explore whether those characteristics hold for millennial lawyers.

First, millennials have been heavily influenced by technology. Most have had the internet since before they were born and came of age with cable television and cell phones. (As an example, I am on the front end of the millennials and I received my first cell phone at 15, which was, not coincidentally, the same time that I received my driver's license.) In at least one survey, millennials said that their technology use was the most defining characteristic of their generation[5] while six-in-ten admit that they get political news on Facebook in a given week.[6]

Historical events have also been formative for millennials, just as they have for any other generation. Millennials experienced 9/11[7] at a critical stage in their development. The oldest millennials were in high school on 9/11. The US was in two wars (Iraq and Afghanistan) for most of their formative years, and the worst economic downturn anyone under 80 can remember peaked the moment millennials became workforce-eligible.[8] These historical events may help explain millennials' significantly lower levels of trust, compared to other generations. Pew Research found that a mere 19 percent of millennials agreed that, generally speaking, most people can be trusted, as compared to 37 percent of the Silent Generation, 40 percent of the Boomer Generation, and 31 percent of Gen X.[9] These lower levels of trust are also likely contributors to millennials' skepticism and demand for transparency and authenticity.[10] Indeed, millennials' demand for authenticity is driving change in brand marketing, making it less about glossy advertising and more about social engagement.[11]

Millennials have also been heavily influenced by social change. They list Barack Obama's election as the second most historic event of their generation, behind 9/11.[12] Other critical events include gay marriage, the shooting at Pulse Nightclub in Orlando, and both the Columbine and Sandy Hook school shootings. They are a giving generation and they often volunteer and give based on causes that inspire them, although typically in modest amounts and to multiple non-profits.[13] Notably, and consistent with their focus on technology, millennials generally use digital technology (websites, social media, mobile platforms, applications) to access information about and donate to causes and non-profits.[14] Some outlets have noted that millennial giving is more likely found on crowdfunding sites.[15] Millennials tend to blend their personal and professional interests for social engagement, getting involved in philanthropic causes with a dual goal of supporting the cause while networking and/or developing skills and expertise that are important to them as professionals.[16]

At a leadership level, millennials' apathy towards hierarchies is well-documented. From a preference for open, breezy, and democratic office environments[17] to their tendency to name people like Mark Zuckerberg as the "face of their generation" (he was the most-cited role model in our millennial lawyer survey too, followed by millennial Nobel Peace Prize winner Malala Yousefi), it is clear that millennials do not buy into the idea that they have to "pay their dues" to get to the top.[18]

Many of these traits can present challenges for law firms. Due to security concerns and risk aversion, law firms are often slower to adopt new technologies. For example, very few use video conferencing with any significant regularity; whereas companies like Google rely on videoconferencing capabilities to connect their global workforce on a regular basis. Both client demands and the need to develop judgment to become a more effective lawyer make it hard to put millennials in the drivers' seat from the moment they walk through the door. The question for law firms is twofold: (1) do millennial lawyers think like their millennial peers and (2) if so, what can law firms do to retain them?

Are millennial lawyers the same and what can law firms do to keep them?

"But what were people saying about the [Greatest Generation] in the early 30s? Not much – a lot of them thought they were pampered and spoiled given how protected they'd been."

Neil Howe, economist and historian who coined the term "millennials"

Three years ago, when Grover Cleveland, Darien Fleming, and I first presented on intergenerational issues, we learned that there was very little research available about millennial lawyers. Given that lawyers tend to differ from the population as a whole,[19] we hypothesized that millennial lawyers might also be different from the millennial population as a whole. To test the hypothesis, in partnership with Above the Law and Ms. JD, we conducted a survey of millennial lawyers. The survey asked participants if they agreed or disagreed with some simple declarative sentences. The results provided insight into how millennial lawyers are both similar to and different from millennials as a whole.[20]

Millennial lawyers display more trust in their firms than millennials generally display for others

First, millennial lawyers express significantly higher levels of trust in their firms than one would expect given the Pew

Research findings that 19 percent of millennials do not trust people generally. Over 50 percent of the millennials we surveyed indicated that they trust their firms.

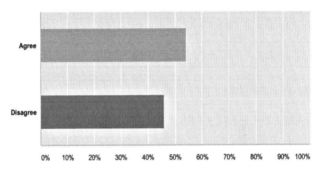

I trust my firm.

Answered: 648   Skipped: 232

Figure 1: I trust my firm

What is driving these results? Do law firms feel more transparent to millennials than the public companies they serve? I doubt it. The more likely explanation for this result is that millennial lawyers are different than their millennial peers in that they are more willing to trust institutions. This is, perhaps, not surprising given the belief that most lawyers have in our justice system and government. That being said, one takeaway from this result for law firm managers is that increased transparency is likely to increase trust among your millennial cohort.

Millennial lawyers recognize that they are responsible for their own career development but law school has not taught them how to be a lawyer and most are not sure where to start
In terms of millennial career development, the survey contained several interesting results. First, millennial lawyers are acutely aware that law school did not prepare them to practice law. Over 70 percent of the respondents disagreed with the statement

that law school prepared them to practice law. Moreover, while nearly 90 percent of our millennial survey respondents said that they knew they were primarily responsible for advancing their own careers, just over 50 percent of them reported that they actually knew what they needed to do to advance their career. These results suggest unease among millennial lawyers about their paths to success and leadership within their firms.

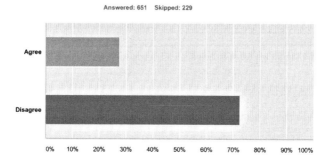

Figure 2: Law school prepared me to practice law

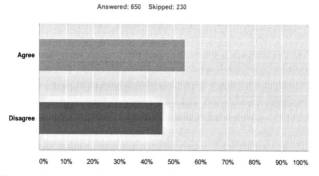

Figure 3: I know what I need to do to advance in my career

These facts provide an incredible opportunity for law firm management because training and mentorship can likely address these issues. It is possible to describe for millennials the skills that they will need to develop to become successful lawyers. Often, firms shy away from creating checklists or even broader documentation about what it takes to be successful as everyone's path to partnership looks different. While that is true, documents can be designed with sufficient caveats to help young lawyers feel like they have more of a roadmap for success. Moreover, providing a list of skills does not mean that an individual lawyer has perfected those skills.

Most millennials view themselves as part of a team; senior lawyers are not their clients

One critical place where millennial lawyers are similar to their peers is in their preference for a flat hierarchy. In response to our statement "Associates should treat senior lawyers as if they were clients", just over 50 percent of the millennial lawyers agreed. Most law firms expect associates to treat more senior lawyers as their own clients and to deliver excellent work product that needs little or no editing. But millennial lawyers view themselves as part of a team and, based on their perception that they have not been well-prepared to practice law, the team member least likely to be able to spot errors. The result is a lot of frustration on the part of their supervisors. These findings may also be contributing to senior lawyer perception that millennials are "lazy".

Flat hierarchies are hard for law firms, particularly Big Law firms which depend on a leveraged model and hierarchy as a business model. But millennials do not have to be in the first chair at trial to believe that they are leading or contributing to the firm. Law firms should look for places where millennials have unique skills to offer or perspectives that they can contribute and create leadership opportunities for millennial lawyers there. For example, many firms invite associates to participate in firm committees; this is a good start. Firms should

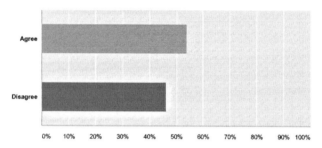

Associates should treat senior lawyers as if they were clients.

Figure 4: Associates should treat senior lawyers as if they were clients

also encourage creating and supporting associate-driven initiatives. These initiatives should have a budget and that budget should be controlled at the associate level. A few good areas to consider for associate-driven initiatives include: social media, diversity (millennials are the most diverse generation to date), and pro bono/philanthropic initiatives. These are topics where millennials are engaged and/or uniquely positioned to provide leadership and support to the firm.

From a day-to-day perspective, I tell the junior lawyers on my teams that they should take ownership of our projects, which includes taking responsibility for our documents, from the content to the citations. I remind them that the leveraged model means they are often closest to the research so they should raise new and unique ideas that they see in their research. We can then discuss why that theory may or may not fit in with the overall case strategy, which has the added bonus of making the junior associates on my team more able to understand our overall case strategy.

I am also open about the fact that I am not infallible and can get citations wrong or read a case aggressively. I encourage junior lawyers on my teams to flag those issues when they see them and then we can discuss why I made the original decision or why I believe that my reading is still accurate. After all, law is about judgment and judgment takes time to develop. I tell young lawyers that we can best develop our own judgment by trying to flex it and then listening to why more experienced lawyers adopted or rejected our approach. In meetings with more senior lawyers, I try to draw out their reasoning for adopting or rejecting a strategy so that other millennial colleagues learn from it as well. The good news is that learning from others' experience is a model that millennials are prone to accept: "[t]hey believe in learning from someone else's experience".[21]

Far from lazy, millennial lawyers recognize that the more they work, the more they learn

Millennial lawyers are not as "lazy" as we may think. Our millennial survey respondents overwhelmingly agreed that the more associates work, the more they learn. They also lamented the fact that they do not get enough feedback on their work. The lack of feedback combined with the recognition that they are (a) primarily responsible for their own careers and (b) sorely unprepared to practice law, likely contributes to millennial discomfort and dissatisfaction in the workplace.

The more I work, the more I learn.

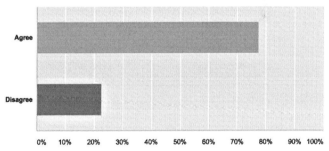

Figure 5: The more I work, the more I learn

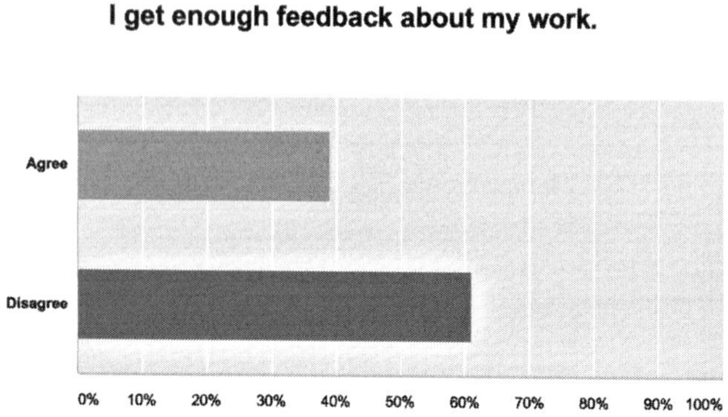

I get enough feedback about my work.

Figure 6: *I get enough feedback about my work*

As a millennial, I *love* feedback. As a millennial supervisor, I *dread* the review period. I take reviews very seriously and want to give honest, constructive, and useful feedback to the attorneys that I work with but review periods always seem to come at a time when we are busiest. Therefore, producing that honest, constructive, and useful feedback tends to happen at 1.00 am. But millennial research shows that millennials seek more regular feedback than any law firm review system allows for. I have made a habit of taking my teams out to lunch to do post-mortems on big filings or to coffee to check in after a big research project. In this way, I provide more regular feedback to individuals on my teams and create a space where they can ask me questions about their performance.

Grover, Darien, and I came up with the idea of "Feedback Tweets" as a more systemic model to promote this kind of interim feedback. At the end of a big project, the system (or an associate) can generate a feedback tweet to send to a supervisor. The tweet could look as simple as Figure 7, and provide a short (character limited) place for the supervisor to give some feedback. More importantly, the tweet provides a reminder for the supervisor and the associate that they should connect to provide more complete feedback while the project is still fresh in everyone's minds.

Provide Immediate Feedback

Figure 7: Instant "feedback tweets"

Feedback is a two-way street so I also encourage millennials to take responsibility for getting their own feedback. To get my own feedback, I go to my supervisors and ask a very simple question: "What are my opportunities for growth between now and the next review period?" I find this question demonstrates that I am open to constructive feedback and helps open my supervisors to giving me the kind of constructive feedback I need to continue to improve. From a firm management perspective, we should develop training programs that encourage our millennial attorneys to actively seek feedback, teaches them *how* to do it, and then lets our supervisors know that they should be engaging with their millennial attorneys for feedback. Encouraging attorneys to seek out feedback is particularly critical for women and diverse attorneys who, research shows, are even less likely to receive the feedback through normal channels.[22]

Millennials are here to stay – How will you engage them?
If they aren't already the majority of your workforce, millennials will be soon. Critically, they are also making their way into leadership at corporate clients, which means that learning to understand them may be important for a firm's future business development. Research shows that millennial lawyers share some of the characteristics of their peers, but not all. Far from sounding the death knell to law firms, millennials could

be engaged, excited firm citizens. The question is how best to leverage their talents and how quickly you will be able to do so. Hopefully this article provides both context as to why your millennial lawyers may act and think as they do and how you can accelerate their growth and leadership potential.

References

1. According to Pew Research, one-in-three American workers as of 2015 were millennials (defined as adults ages 18–34 in 2015), surpassing Gen X to become the largest share of the American workforce. See Fry, R. *Milllennials Surpass Gen Xers as the Largest Generation in the U.S. Labor Force*, Pew Research, 11 May 2015. Available at: http://www. pewresearch.org/fact-tank/2015/05/11/millennials-surpass-gen-xers-as-the-largest-generation-in-u-s-labor-force/.

2. Many in my generation hate the word "millennial" and actively avoid being associated with it. One study estimated that as many as two-thirds of us reject the term. See Berman J. "Many Millennials Hate Being Called 'Millennial'", MarketWatch. Available at: http://www.marketwatch. com/story/many-millennials-hate-being-called-millennial-2015-05-18, 30 May 2015. I understand why so many in my generation reject the term; I do not believe "lazy, coddled, and entitled" describes me either. However, I fall into the camp of millennials who actively seek to reclaim the word and everything it represents about our generation. As a result, I will use "millennial" throughout this article but not before cautioning managers that my peers may not embrace the word and you may not want to use it when speaking to and training millennials.

3. Grover Cleveland is an attorney, speaker, and author of *Swimming Lessons for Baby Sharks*, a career advice book for young lawyers. Darien Fleming is a former law firm professional development manager and the CEO and Executive Coach behind I'M Possible.

4. This is the title of Lauren Stiller Rikleen's book on managing millennials, which was itself inspired by a millennial.

5. See Nielsen, *Millennials: Technology = Social Connection*, 26 February 2014. Available at: http://www.nielsen.com/us/en/insights/news/2014/ millennials-technology-social-connection.html?afflt=ntrt15340001&afflt _uid=uksJCC5n9Lg.gFu77BYnRTrSmOnwXNlaQchDiTpLwInu&afflt _uid_2=AFFLT_ID_2.

6. See Gao, G. *15 Striking Findings from 2015*, Pew Research, 22 December 2015. Available at: http://www.pewresearch.org/fact-tank/ 2015/12/22/15-striking-findings-from-2015/.

7. Not surprisingly, most Americans include the September 11th terror attacks as one of the ten most significant events in their lifetimes. See

Deane, C., Duggan, M. and Morin, R. *Americans Name the 10 Most Significant Historic Events of Their Lifetimes*, Pew Research, 15 December 2016. Available at: http://www.people-press.org/2016/12/15/americans-name-the-10-most-significant-historic-events-of-their-lifetimes/ (hereinafter "Pew Top Ten").

8. Ibid. Notably, while millennials list the Great Recession among the top ten events of their lifetimes, no other generation agreed which suggests that the effects of the recession may have been felt more strongly by millennials, either because of their own experiences or perhaps because of their fears about the experiences of their parents.

9. Pew Research Center, *Millennials Less Trusting of Others*, 5 March 2014. Available at: http://www.pewsocialtrends.org/2014/03/07/millennials-in-adulthood/sdt-next-america-03-07-2014-0-05/.

10. See Landrum, S. "4 Things Millennials Value in Their Professional Lives", *Forbes*, 22 February 2017. Available at: https://www.forbes.com/sites/sarahlandrum/2017/02/22/how-companies-are-saving-money-and-making-millennials-happier/#10a966c25917.

11. See Tyson, M. "Millennials Want Brands to be More Authentic. Here's Why That Matters", the *Huffington Post*, 20 January 2017. Available at http://www.huffingtonpost.com/matthew-tyson/millennials-want-brands-t_b_9032718.html.

12. Pew Top Ten, *supra* n. 7.

13. Achieve, *Cause, Influence & the Workplace The Millennial Impact Report Retrospective: Five Years of Trends*, 2016. Available at: http://achievemulti.wpengine.com/mi/files/2016/11/FiveYearRecap_MIR_Achieve.pdf (hereinafter "Achieve").

14. Ibid.

15. Bourque, A. "Are Millennials the Most Generous Generation?", *Entrepreneur*, 29 March 2016. Available at: https://www.entrepreneur.com/article/271466.

16. Achieve, *supra* n.11.

17. See Schulte, B. "Millennials Want an End to Hierarchies in the Workplace", *Chicago Tribune*, 21 June 2015, available at: http://www.chicagotribune.com/dp-millennials-want-an-end-to-hierarchies-in-the-workplace-20150622-story.html.

18. See generally Stahl, A. "A Millennial Manifesto: Why Gen Y Will Change the World", *Forbes*, 28 April 2016. Available at: https://www.forbes.com/sites/ashleystahl/2016/04/28/a-millennial-manifesto/#24b0b0252616.

19. Compare American Bar Assoc. *Lawyer Demographics*, 2015, available at: https://www.americanbar.org/content/dam/aba/administrative/market_research/lawyer-demographics-tables-2015.authcheckdam.pdf with United States Census Bureau, *Quick Facts United States,* 2015. Available at: https://www.census.gov/quickfacts/table/PST045216/00.

20. As part of the original survey, we presented the same sentences to

professional development managers, but asked them to agree or disagree based on their subjective belief about what their millennial associates would say. Those results are not reported in this article but I think it is important to note that, almost without exception, professional development managers had a more negative perception of what they thought their millennial associates would say than what the millennial associates actually said. This suggests that the perceptions of millennial associates may be driven by negative reports in the media and/or generalizations of a few bad experiences to all millennial attorneys. Notably, many millennials have written that they do not believe the negative perceptions popularized by the media describe them or their friends. For one example of a millennial lawyer's perception, see Abboud, N. "The Gen Why Lawyer: How Millennials Are Changing the Legal Workplace", *Ms. JD*, 5 May 2016. Available at http://ms-jd.org/blog/article/the-gen-why-lawyer-how-millennials-are-changing-the-legal-workplace.

21. See Gillaspie, D. "5 Ways Millennials Are Like No Generation Before Them", *Entrepreneur*, 13 March 2015, available at: https://www.entrepreneur.com/article/243862.

22. See Jaffe, A., Chediak, G., Tudor, M. , Douglas, E., Gordon, R., Rica, L., and Robinson, S. "Retaining and Advancing Women in National Law Firms", Stanford Law School Women in Law Policy Lab Practicum, 28, May 2016. Available at: https://law.stanford.edu/wp-content/uploads/2016/05/Women-in-Law-White-Paper-FINAL-May-31-2016.pdf (noting that women and minorities are more likely to receive comments related to their team rather than their individual accomplishments).

Chapter 6:
Getting down to business development – What works for women?

By *Carol Frohlinger, Negotiating Women Inc.*

> *"At the end of the day, the firms that continue to prosper will most likely be those that are able to adapt most successfully to the evolving demands of their clients and the changed conditions of the marketplace. Those firms that are unable to do so will most likely become endangered species".*[1]

The "new normal" is a term in business and economics that refers to financial conditions following the financial crisis of 2007–2008 and the aftermath of the 2008–2012 global recession. Although I can't take credit for coining the term, I think it's right on point to describe the substantial impact the Great Recession had on professional services firms.

Consider the following:

- Clients, under increasing pressure to contain costs, are keeping more work in-house, and, when they do send work out, they pay more attention to the "value" they receive.

- Evaluation criteria used to hire firms initially, as well as to make decisions about whether to continue to work with them on an ongoing basis, have become more stringent.

- Increased competition, from traditional competitors as well as from new entrants to the market and technological advances, make it more challenging to grow revenue.

As pressures continue to mount, law firms increasingly demand that equity partners (and those who aspire to become equity partners) generate revenue. Few would disagree – the bottom line is, originating business effectively and efficiently is no longer a "nice to have", it is an essential survival skill. Although the mandate to build business is clear, less well-defined are the activities that work, particularly those that work for women.

Based on research reported and discussed in "Business Development In The 'New Normal': Factors That Correlate With Origination For Law Firm Male Equity Partners And For Female Equity Partners",[2] this article will offer prescriptive advice women can apply to enhance their business development results.[3] It is critically important to note that *second generation gender issues* (the powerful yet often unexamined barriers women face that arise from either cultural beliefs about gender – gender stereotypes – or embedded workplace structures, practices, and patterns of interaction that inadvertently favor men[4] explain a great deal of the revenue origination gap that exists between men and women.[5] Clearly, a dual-pronged approach – to identify and remedy systemic issues as well as to support women lawyers to enhance their business development skills – is required to solve the problem.[6] However, since there seems to be scant commitment on the part of law firms to disrupt the status quo by addressing the systemic issues, individual women must make good decisions regarding the approach they will take to business development. The objective of this article is to synthesize the study's findings to assist women to do just that.

What should women keep doing?
Building external referral relationships
Referrals matter a great deal; clients are seeking "trusted advisors". When the right people are willing to put their credibility on the line on your behalf by making a strategic introduction, it can get you into the client's consideration set. Cultivate your

existing referral sources by finding ways to reciprocate. Always be on the lookout for appropriate additions to your referral network.

Asking clients for new matters

Clients with whom you have worked are natural sources of new work; they know the value you provide. Don't make the mistake of thinking that they know you want additional work and will offer you the opportunity to bid on it when they have it; instead, ask in a relationship-oriented way, at suitable intervals.

Asking clients for introductions

As with asking clients for new matters, asking clients for introductions to their colleagues or their contacts is an effective and efficient way to generate originations. The right to ask is a natural outcome of excellent client service. Consider offering to ghost draft an email they can edit (or not!) and send it to save them time and effort.

Taking the perspective of others

Success in business development requires that the focus be on the client rather than on you. It is critical that you know the answers to questions like those that follow: what are the decision-makers thinking? What concerns might they have about hiring you? How can you eliminate (or at least mitigate) their concerns?

Persuading clients and prospects they will benefit from the services you provide

If potential clients don't see a clear benefit to the services you provide and to working with you specifically, they will not make the decision to hire you. You must clearly articulate why and how you are the best possible choice of counsel.

This can be challenging for some women who are not comfortable with self-promotion. And "bragging" can trigger backlash when women do it. The solution? Demonstrate your legal expertise and your business acumen in a style that is comfortable for you. Don't assume that people will figure it out themselves – find a way to help them to see the value you bring to them and their organizations.

What should women do more of?
Getting in the right frame of mind
Accept that building a book of business is necessary to become an equity partner, to stay one, or to move laterally. Of course, there are other choices you can take if BD isn't something you want to do. Like it or not, being a talented lawyer is necessary but not sufficient in today's economic climate for equity partners, except in rare cases. The good news is that there are many ways to successfully build business.

Seek out successful rainmakers (both men and women) as role models and mentors. Don't just take their advice – ask them to let you observe them in action as appropriate. Don't limit yourself – develop a few mentoring relationships and learn from each of them.

Develop your own plan about how you will be successful at BD – and work it!

Becoming "the" (or at least "a") request for proposal (RFP) go-to person
Although participating in RFPs is one activity that is currently working for women, you might take your participation to the next level by becoming known as an "expert" at writing proposals that win work. This expertise should include identifying the RFPs that don't deserve a great deal of time or effort and guiding others to accept your recommendations.

Don't get stuck doing the "invisible work"[7] without negotiating for an appropriate share of the credit for managing the RFP process and the origination credit if the firm wins the work.

Negotiating for the "right" amount of BD resources
Figure out the BD budget that others get, plan a strategy, and

ask those with decision-making authority for what you need. Keep in mind, however, that you may anticipate pushback so you need to proceed with caution.

Explore whether you can collaborate with others (either inside the firm, with partners whose clients overlap with your potential clients, or with external partners) to hold events.

Bouncing back consciously
Those who bounce back quickly (and the research shows women do) when BD activities fail are more successful at generating revenue. That's no surprise! Because it is so much more challenging for women to generate originations, we encourage you to take things one step further to build your "grit" and resiliency muscles.[8]

Building referral relationships with other firm partners
Referrals from others in different practice areas and firm offices are an excellent way to build business. Be sure that your colleagues know what you do and why they should trust you by referring work to you. When you make a referral to a colleague, be sure you set the expectation that you will be expecting a referral back, as appropriate.

Aspiring to leadership positions in the firm
Being in a leadership role in your firm gives you access to information you wouldn't normally know and boosts your credibility. Both are important to originating business. Getting appointed to formal leadership positions (to the "right" committees, as a practice leader, or as an office managing partner) can be a challenge for women for many complicated reasons, among them the fact that the selection of those leadership roles is correlated to the size of one's book of business.

Meeting with clients annually
Even if you think that things are going well with a client relationship, make the time to have a formal meeting annually to

assess what's working and what's not. Be sure to include all stakeholders. You will probably learn a lot and may uncover other opportunities to work with the client.

Making sure clients know your team members

In a client service culture, making sure that clients know – and have the opportunity to work with – others on your team is critical. It also helps you to free up time to focus on other important activities.

What should women do less of?

Attending pitch meetings arranged by others

Unless you have negotiated a role at the meeting, appropriate credit for attending, and a share of the work that results from it, think twice before going. If you decide to attend a pitch meeting as a quid pro quo to support someone who has supported you at a pitch meeting or to model how to conduct an effective client meeting for a less experienced lawyer, participating may be the right thing to do. Otherwise, arrange your own pitch meetings and invite other partners as suitable or re-allocate your time to BD activities that will build your business.

Attending the wrong BD training

Unless it's designed with the particular challenges women face vis a vis BD, not only could this training be a waste of your time, but you may even get bad advice – techniques that are effective for men often backfire when women use them. Negotiate to have the firm invest in the right kind and type of BD training.[9]

References

1. 2017 Report on the State of the Legal Market, The Center for the Study of the Legal Profession at Georgetown University Law Center and Thomson Reuters Legal Executive Institute.
2. Frohlinger, C., "Business Development In The 'New Normal': Factors That Correlate With Origination For Law Firm Male Equity Partners And For Female Equity Partners", whitepaper originally published by the Thomson Reuters Legal Executive Institute, October 2015. Available at: http://legalexecutiveinstitute.com/

what-does-origination-success-look-like-for-male-and-female-equity-partners/. See Appendix A for a summary of the results.

3. Ibid. Factors were defined as specific attitudes, activities, roles and resources affect business origination. They help attorneys to generate new work which, in turn, affects not only compensation but also their ability to assume leadership roles within their firms. These factors were categorized as either "firm based factors" (FBFs) – those derived from association with a firm – or "self-generated factors" (SGFs) – those resulting from individual engagement with the business development process.

4. Sturm, S. "Second Generation Employment Discrimination: A Structural Approach" *Columbia Law Review*, Vol. 101, No. 1, April 2001. See also Kolb, D. M., Williams, J. and Frohlinger, C. *Her Place at The Table: A Woman's Guide to Negotiating Five Key Challenges to Leadership Success*, San Francisco: Jossey & Bass, 2010.

5. For a detailed analysis of ways SGGI affect women vis a vis business development, see Frohlinger, C. and Schonholtz, M. B. "Scaling the Rainbow: The Future for Women and Business Development", originally published in *Breaking Barriers: Promoting and Retaining Women in the Legal Profession* by ARK Group in association with *Managing Partner*, 2014.

6. See "The Five Year Moment", (https://legaltalentlab.app.box.com/v/2016hackathon/1/8809339838/73319480565/1), one of the winning ideas generated by The Women in Law Hackathon (http://www.diversitylab.com/hackathons). The Women in Law Hackathon is a Shark Tank style pitch competition created by the Diversity Lab in collaboration with Stanford Law School and Bloomberg Law. Carol Frohlinger served as an advisor to this team.

7. Joyce K. Fletcher defines "invisible work" as work that contributes to the organization's success but does not get much, if any, notice or recognition. Consequently, it is neither highly valued nor rewarded. See Fletcher, J. K. *Disappearing Acts: Gender, Power, And Relational Practice at Work*, Boston: MIT Press, 1999.

8. For further information, see the work of Dr. Angela Duckworth. You can view her TED Talk here: https://www.ted.com/talks/angela_lee_duckworth_grit_the_power_of_passion_and_perseverance.

9   Frohlinger, supra, note 4.

Appendix A: Summary of "Business Development in the 'New Normal'"

"Business Development in the 'New Normal': Factors that Correlate with Origination for Law Firm Male Equity Partners and for Female Equity Partners" was originally published by the Thomson Reuters Legal Executive Institute in October 2015.

Data collected from 437 male and female equity partners in law firms of all sizes across the US during the period from 2011–2013 categorized 16 factors that result in business origination into one of two classifications – those derived from association with a firm (firm-based factors) or those resulting from individual engagement with the business development process (self-generated factors).

The results were analyzed separately for male equity partners and female equity partners (see Figure 1 for a chart providing more detailed information). The male equity partners' originations were positively correlated with five of the eight firm-based factors; whereas female equity partners' originations were correlated with two of the eight firm-based factors, one being negatively associated.

When self-generated factors were analyzed, the results showed that male equity partners' originations were positively correlated with three of the eight self-generated factors and that female equity partners' originations were positively correlated with five of the eight factors.

Only two factors – one firm-based, the other self-generated – were correlated with origination for both male equity partners and female equity partners. Finally, we found that two factors did not correlate with origination for either male equity partners or female equity partners.

The quantitative data was supplemented by qualitative data gathered by the author during in-depth interviews with 60 AmLaw 100 and AmLaw 200 female equity partners during 2013–2105 and as a result of conducting workshops on the topics of business development or negotiation with hundreds of other women in professional services over the last 12 years.

Firm based factors

Firm based factors (FBFs) result from having a position in a law firm. The law firm role offers access to business development (BD) resources as well as the opportunity to perform BD activities. Firm based factors are further categorized as either "direct" or "indirect".

Direct firm based factors

These activities connect attorneys with current clients, prospects, and referral sources and can directly lead to new business. Direct FBFs include:

- Participation in requests for proposals (RFPs);
- Participation in pitch groups;
- Internal referrals from firm partners; and
- Receiving the "right" amount of financial support for BD activities.

Indirect firm based factors

Although indirect firm based factors do not put attorneys in situations that are likely to directly lead to new business, they are nonetheless very helpful to build revenue. Indirect FBFs include:

- Holding leadership positions in the firm;
- Building referral relationships;
- Cross-selling opportunities; and
- Receiving BD training, coaching, and mentoring.

Self-generated factors

Self-generated factors (SGFs) are relationship building and selling skills related to an individual's personality traits, skills, and behaviors. Affiliation with a law firm, other than the indirect benefits resulting from the firm's overall branding and marketing efforts, is irrelevant. Self-generated factors are further categorized as either "external" or "internal".

External self-generated factors

External SGFs include:

- Focusing on client service;
- Building client relationships by meeting regularly;
- Asking clients for additional work; and
- Asking clients for referrals.

It is an axiom that future business from clients depends on their satisfaction levels with past delivery of services. It is also true that people hire lawyers they like and trust. Finally, asking for work and soliciting referrals are among the behaviors incontrovertibly linked to building revenue.

Internal self-generated factors

Internal SGFs include:

- Empathy;
- Persuasiveness;
- Resiliency; and
- Engagement with BD activities and motivation to succeed.

Empathy is the ability to take the perspective of others. In other studies, empathy, strong BD motivation, and resiliency all correlate with rainmaking. Persuasiveness is the skill of persuading clients and prospects that they will benefit from using the attorney's services. Resiliency refers to individuals who quickly rebound and continue BD activities even when they were not successful in their prior efforts; resiliency keeps the search for new business a continuous activity. Perseverance when BD efforts are unsuccessful is a form of resiliency. Resiliency and perseverance have been characterized as "grittiness", defined as "…the tendency to sustain interest in and effort toward very long-term goals". Finally, people are successful at BD when they are committed to make the requisite effort and are driven to succeed.

Female equity partners	Both	Male equity partners
External self-generated questions ● Asking clients for new matters ● Asking clients for introductions	Direct firm-based factors ● Participating in RFPs	Direct firm-based factors ● Participating in pitch teams ● Receiving the right amount of BD resources
Internal self-generated factors ● Taking the perspectives of others ● Being skillful at persuading clients and prospects they will benefit from services	Internal self-generated factors ● Bouncing back quickly when BD activities fail	Indirect firm-based factors ● Holding a leadership position ● Receiving training and mentoring for BD activities and skills
		External self-generated factors ● Meeting with clients in person annually
		Internal self-generated factors ● Being strongly motivated to generate significant new work for others and myself

Figure 1: Factors correlated to origination
Note that neither the direct firm-based factor of "Receiving referrals from other partners" nor the indirect firm-based factor of "Cross-selling to existing clients" correlated with origination for either male equity partners or female equity partners.

Chapter 7:
Striking the self-promotion balance – Demonstrating your value without being the obnoxious one in the room

By Debbie Epstein Henry, DEH Consulting, Speaking, Writing; co-founder and managing director of Bliss Lawyers

You know those people at the office meetings and cocktail parties who tell you how great they are. You remember those instances of people bragging and how off-putting it was. In fact, you are struck by how vivid those impressions are and how those moments stay with you. The idea of coming off that self-serving, arrogant, or entitled is embarrassing to you. You've sworn to yourself to never be those people.

So why read an article on self-promotion? Perhaps because instinctively you know that it's important. Whether you are aspiring for a promotion, leadership opportunity, or to get credit for managing a team or client matter, self-promotion is a critical skill you need to hone. That's because self-promotion, when done effectively, is not about aggressively seeking credit for something you don't deserve and offending people along the way. It's about demonstrating your value and opening yourself up to opportunities without being transparent or manipulative. Bottom line is if you are not able to communicate your value, you run the risk of being overlooked.

Yet even if you are convinced that self-promotion is justified and necessary, it doesn't mean you are comfortable doing it. Many people are afraid to self-promote. They worry it is obvious and awkward. They don't want to be perceived as bragging. They may feel unworthy. Or, even if they know they have to do it, they may be too self-conscious to claim their contributions. Some worry that by self-promoting, they are demanding too much and it may be an imposition on others to enlist them for help. They also don't want to battle their colleagues for a position or recognition. Others worry they are not savvy enough to navigate the internal politics of self-promoting in their workplace or network.

Women, in particular, often think their accomplishments should speak for themselves. This belief, however, comes at a cost. "Success, it turns out, correlates just as closely with confidence as it does with competence."[1] In other words, it's not enough to be good. Your projected confidence is just as important in how you are evaluated in the workplace as your actual competence and ability to deliver top-notch work.

But even if you know that you need to more effectively convey your value, how do you get there? How do you strike that balance between demonstrating your contribution while not being that obnoxious person in the room? Here are the steps that should help:

1. Be great

If you are going to self-promote, you want to be sure that you have a legitimate basis for doing so. It requires you to be indispensable to your colleagues and clients. It also is important that you understand your value and know how it will bring a significant benefit to others.

2. Be prepared

Know your stuff cold. Be practiced and ready to communicate your value. Perfect an elevator speech. Be prepared to track your contributions and communicate them. If that is at an annual review, go to that review with your own agenda and punch list of what you have done and what you hope to do next. But don't wait for an annual review because it will be too late. Regular communication and solicitation of feedback is critical in demonstrating your value. Pre-meetings help with preparation too. These informal, smaller meetings allow you to assess your colleagues' inclinations before you are in a larger group.

3. Observe others

Knowing and reading your audience is critical to effective self-promotion. Study up on who will be in the room in advance. Assess commonalities and areas that may create tension to position your recommendations so they will be received in a favorable way. Evaluate what makes others' effective, what they do that would work for you, and what you don't like and why. Access self-promoters who you think are effective, ask them directly what they do and how they cultivated their skill.

4. Credit others

It is important to acknowledge others' contributions. An audience is more receptive to someone seeking self-recognition when that person acknowledges the expertise and contributions of others. Citing others' work is a way to do that and it should not matter if that person is a competitor. In fact, citing a competitor may demonstrate not only proper attribution but also a generous spirit and important prioritization to aspire to a larger goal or cause, beyond yourself. That said, you don't want to fawn or come off as disingenuous or someone who is seeking some sort of quid pro quo acknowledgement.

5. Benefit others

If you have the ability to align your self-promotion for the benefit of your employer or another organization or individual, all the better. Forward your boss a congratulatory email from a client and accompany the email with a cover note indicating that you think now is the time to grow the relationship with the client. You will be seen by your boss as someone who is thinking about the larger goal of the company's success rather than simply sharing an accolade. Pair self-promotion with being a helpful resource. So, if you want the exposure to appear before a client and you can provide an expertise that is valuable to them, it will be an opportunity for you to self-promote as well as be a resource. Promote others where you can, too. But be sure these individuals are worthy of your praise because you are putting your reputation on the line in promoting them. Sometimes, promoting others will result in that person becoming what I call a "promotion buddy" who can in turn recommend you for opportunities as well. Promotion by others is often better received as more legitimate and not seemingly self-interested.

6. Get help

Seek out sponsors and mentors who can help with your promotion. They may provide advice about how to self-promote effectively. If they know your work and your organization, they will be more helpful in enabling you to navigate the right tone and approach. If the people you seek out for advice are ones who can promote on your behalf, that is an added benefit. However, be careful not to ask for too much, especially when involving personal contacts for a business purpose. You need to be willing to tap into your personal network yet be sensitive to avoid any awkwardness if the business opportunity does not come to fruition.

7. Own it

An important part of self-promotion is simply taking credit where credit is due. Many people have trouble doing this and when they are acknowledged, they deflect the compliment or redirect it in some other way. While it is gracious to acknowledge other contributors, it is also important to unapologetically say "thank you". If you are in a setting where you are being recognized and the custom is for someone to share your accomplishments, follow protocol and allow that information to be shared. If you are asked to explain why you are suited for an opportunity, take a factual approach. Rather than say "I am a great leader", provide an example, with demonstrated facts, of when you led a team successfully.

8. Take risks

Self-promotion involves taking some professional risks. For example, you may have to be confrontational with a colleague who is diminishing your contribution or take a stand on an important project that is being sidelined. Evaluating whether it is appropriate to take these risks is often a separate process in and of itself.[2] But when contemplating the risk in self-promotion, you must also consider the risk of inaction.

9. Make the ask

Effective self-promotion may require making an ask of someone. As a junior person, maybe you will want to ask to shadow a senior leader you admire to gain learning and exposure. Asking often involves understanding the challenges a person or group is facing and determining how you can be helpful. Then it may involve offering yourself as a resource and in turn, self-promoting by being the one to address the need. Practice and role play before making an ask. An initial ask may need to be small and specific. Expect that your request and effort to self-promote may be declined. You will then need to learn how to ask again. Evaluate whether and when it is appropriate to make another ask and consider factors including new circumstances, passage of time, change in decision-makers, etc.

10. Show initiative

Often the best way to self-promote is to stand out. This may involve volunteering for a project when no one else is raising their hand. Or, maybe it is preparing a presentation or punch list of recommendations when it's not expected or requested. Showing initiative may result in you becoming a point person in an area where you have been struggling to distinguish yourself or perhaps it will get you one-on-one exposure with a senior leader with whom you've been trying to establish a rapport.

11. Pay attention to the details

When you are self-promoting, just like any other form of communication, the delivery and how you convey your message is critical. You need to frame your request to maximize the likelihood of it being received positively. Be aware of your physical stance and be thoughtful about your tone. You want to convey a commanding presence but also one that is inviting and friendly. Make eye contact and demonstrate sincerity and directness. Be sure you have the right audience – decision-makers who can evaluate your desire to advance or seek a new opportunity. Also, ensure that you are in the right venue. Your audience should be comfortable and open to receiving your information. Consider the timing too. Make sure your audience has the time to reflect on the information you share.

12. Understand you will mess up

You are not perfect and you will make mistakes in attempting to self-promote. You may even jeopardize a valuable relationship that you won't be able to reconcile. Recognize and apologize when you have gone too far. Be honest and show humility when you have over-stepped. Also, acknowledge shameless self-promotion and self-interest. Solicit feedback on how you are doing in striking the self-promotion balance. This may take the form of anonymous written evaluations. If you have a small circle of trusted advisors who can provide candid feedback, seek it out.

13. Develop a signature

In the end, the best way to demonstrate your value is to be original. For some of you, that may mean telling stories. For others, it may be natural to use humor or self-deprecation. Ideally, you want to be likeable and fun. And, the bottom line is you want to be memorable and make it personal.

The goal of effective self-promotion is to master the elusive challenge of being a team player while seeking recognition for your role. If you are able to identify techniques that are unique to you that demonstrate your contribution, you will gain the recognition you both need and deserve.

This article was originally published in the Spring 2017 issue of the ACC Chicago Newsletter.

References

1. Kay, K. and Shipman, C., "The Confidence Gap", *The Atlantic*, May 2014.
2. See generally Henry, D. E. "Developing a Healthy Appetite for Risk in Your Career", in *A publication of the Corporate Counsel Section of the New York State Bar Association,* Vol.34 No.2, Fall 2016.

Chapter 8:
Does size really matter?

By Cathy Fleming, partner at Fleming.Ruvoldt PLLC

Does size really matter? The potential answer to that question, in its traditional context, has been the cause of male anxiety for generations for which no cure has been found. The value of the obsession with size can be measured by the billions of dollars spent each year in the diet industry. In the business of law, the question drives both sexes to the pharmacist for Xanax or to the local bar for a drink.

A wise mentor told me in my early years of trying to build a practice that a person with a license to practice law need never starve. That simple truth – that if my comfortable world at a traditional law firm crumbled I could practice law from my kitchen and pay my bills – has been a core comfort to me for some 30 years. It is absolutely true.

This chapter is not based on scientific analysis nor is it based on empirical studies over time. Rather, it is founded on personal experiences and observations practicing law for some 38 years. This chapter describes my reality as I have lived it as:

1.   An associate at a big firm (four years);

2.   An Assistant United States Attorney, including as a chief (five years);

3.   A founding partner of a "boutique" litigation firm with three other former federal prosecutors (10 years);

4.   A contract partner at a midsize New York City firm (two years); and

5. An equity partner at several AmLaw 200 firms in New York, including as chair of the White Collar Group at one firm and partner-in-charge of the New York City office of another (15 years).

Two years ago, I left "Big Law" and joined a two-partner fledgling law firm. Now the firm has nine full-time attorneys and two paralegals, as well as a phalanx of contract attorneys and paralegals (currently 16) to handle our caseload. The firm is multilingual and has open matters across three continents. The boutique firm I chose does not look small now.

So does size matter? For me, it does not. For the wise client it should not. I have truly liked, and even loved, each and every place I have practiced. There have been good and bad aspects to each. My all-time favorite – federal prosecutor – was by far the lowest paying legal job I have had since graduating from law school. It was, however, where I learned to try a case and where I established lifelong and career-rich friendships and relationships. A small firm, especially one you run and own, gives you more control over your life and schedule (subject to client demands, of course), but it requires more administrative time, more soup-to-nuts work (e.g. no office services departments to collate briefs on the weekends), and commands a closer watch on cash flow and finances. Not once at Big Law did my office manager warn me that if we didn't collect receivables we would need to tap the credit line to make payroll. (Fortunately, that has not occurred since 1989.) On the plus side, however, when there is a particularly good quarter, that reward can be taken immediately. In Big Law there were many more compartmentalized and 24/7 support services. Others took care of the web page, reception desk coverage, banking reconciliations, etc. In part, the price of all this support was company politics: lots of politics. Others decided my annual compensation and sometimes vetoed cases I wanted to take. Worse were the "conflicts": actual, potential, or imagined ("we may get to represent this bank sometime in the future"). Frequently in attempting to bring in a new matter, an obstacle course of objections existed as a prelude to approval. While I truly believe that my partners were lovely and well-intentioned people, I could not always agree with them on how the firm should be run. More importantly, I did not always like the control they had over my caseload, my practice, and to some extent my life. I have a white collar practice which sometimes ends up with an unpaid receivable. In a small firm, where decision making is much simpler – we discuss and decide an issue over breakfast – I, with the benefit of smart and reasoned thinking of supportive partners, make the choice as to what cases to take and I live with the consequences. In Big Law, what may be a good choice for the firm as a whole – which I understand and accept – may not be a good choice for me. Part of my ability to land desirable cases has been success in high profile, *New York Times* front-page cases, which were not always financially lucrative. Part of my satisfaction in being a lawyer has been the ability to represent someone who couldn't afford to pay what it costs to defend a case, but who richly (pun intended) deserved to be defended.

Here is the key to independence: having a book of business. The reason I have been able to move, and frankly to be successful, is that after I left the government in 1987, I learned to develop, market, and attract clients. A book of business is where size in fact matters. (Candor requires me to acknowledge my 28-year relationship with my wonderful and loyal assistant, Annie, who has (almost always cheerfully) moved with me each time and who helps me manage the practice.)

Let me say it again. In order to have control over her own destiny, a lawyer must have her own book of business. She must be able to support herself. Anyone can do it. Really.

One chapter cannot teach you how to develop a book of business. I am a believer in coaches to help lawyers grow their business. I am the lawyer I am today because of the generosity of the great lawyers who mentored me. I willingly embrace my responsibility to pay that mentoring forward. I, and more importantly my clients, have benefited greatly from a more than

20-year team practice. While the amount of business has fluctuated up and down over the years, business has always been there. Fortunately, I have always earned a very comfortable living doing good cases for great clients. In this chapter, briefly, are some suggestions to attract clients, as well as some mistakes I see struggling lawyers make repeatedly. The lawyers in small firms are generally much better marketers than the majority of attorneys in Big Law: they have to be or they starve.

Mistake #1: Always believing what Big Law managers tell you

Too often, we see promising young lawyers in Big Law assigned to specialized departments working on large matters for others. They stay there complacent, fed work, for years. They may even become service partners. The Great Lie is: "Work hard, we will make you a partner and you will inherit clients." The partners who say it may even mean it when they say it. But it is almost never true. This is the legal urban myth version of "the check is in the mail" or "your car will be ready tomorrow". It *could* happen, but it generally does not. Inevitably, the time comes when a firm decides to tighten its figurative belt and the first to be let go are the higher paid attorneys who do not produce business. The legal market is saturated with 12-year lawyers with specialized backgrounds who were paid significant salaries, and who have no or little business and no or little experience in other areas. They are forced to reinvent themselves. These candidates are unmarketable without reinvention. The lesson is simply "nurture your own career path".

Mistake #2: Not marketing on a daily basis

We all get very busy. It is important to market, even when working 14-hour days. Those busy periods end. Marketing must be a daily habit, like brushing your teeth, even if it is an email, a note, a phone call, or a targeted lunch. My team partner is a genius at marketing. I often kid him that if he attends a funeral, he returns with a client. The lesson is simply that "marketing is a daily habit".

Mistake #3: Targeting the wrong clients

A young lawyer is not likely to bag General Motors as her first client. Do your research for the area in which you practice and consider the size client you appropriately can serve. Find touch points for that client. Be creative. Do not do what everyone else does. General Counsels do not need "client alerts" every day from 100 law firms. Stand out from the crowd. The lesson simply is "pick a segment to serve and differentiate yourself from your competition".

Mistake #4: Not making sure you are happy

I love what I do. Love it. (Most of the time.) What we do is hard and takes hours and dedication. I cannot imagine devoting the time and energy to being a lawyer if I didn't enjoy the work, the challenges, the clients, and my colleagues. If you are not happy with your position, change it. It doesn't mean you have to change jobs, although that might be the result. It might be as small a tweak as seeking work or clients in a new area. It might mean accepting pro bono work in a field for which you feel a passion. It might be joining a bar association or participating in an Inn of Court or teaching CLE courses. Being active in the National Association of Women Lawyers (NAWL) was another career highlight for me. And teaching and mentoring women has been a passion and a work of love for me. The lesson simply is "working at your passion makes you passionate about your work".

Mistake #5: Thinking Big Law is the only source of excellent lawyers

There is real snobbery among the AmLaw 100 that they are the exclusive band of excellent lawyers out there. Sorry folks, that view is undeserved. While it certainly boasts many wonderful lawyers, Big Law also has its share of mediocre, and even poor, lawyers lurking within its halls. Small firms have excellent lawyers too (and mediocre ones as well). As the economy has worsened, clients have become cognizant of this fact. Big Law certainly garners large, high-paying clients, "bet the farm" cases, and significant deals. Small firms also attract great clients, interesting and significant matters, and high-paying clients. My practice has not changed substantially, even as my offices changed; I have the same clients, same billing rates, and same kinds of matters. My earnings are on a par with equity partnership compensation at Big Law. My case origination revenue in 2016 was among my highest years. I do, however, have the ability to decide what cases I choose to take, and what fees I choose to charge. We actually can and do employ alternative fee arrangements. We are flexible with our clients. The lesson simply is "be excellent and act accordingly".

Mistake #6: Believing that clients will come to you just because you are a good lawyer

There are lots and lots of really excellent lawyers. Excellence is presumed. Why are you, among all the truly fine lawyers, the one that a client should choose? The first step is meeting the potential buyer of our services and the second is convincing her that you, above all others, are the right choice. I represent people and entities going through some of the darkest, most difficult periods of their lives. It is the highest compliment I receive that among many competent, good lawyers, a client chooses me for that journey. Why? I think it is because a client knows I care, I believe, and I will do everything lawfully and ethically in my power to help them. In other words, the client trusts me. And I do everything I can do to earn and keep that trust. The lesson simply is "deserve and earn your clients' confidence".

Mistake #7: Not respecting adequately the referring source of business

I am genuinely grateful that others consider me capable and the correct choice for doing legal work for their clients, family, and friends. I make sure that I make the person – usually a lawyer – who recommended me look good. I never "poach"; I keep the lawyer apprised of the matter, and I look for *appropriate* opportunities to return the referral. Most importantly, I do a great job for the person or company they have referred. The lesson simply is "respect those who feed you, they are your friends".

Conclusion

Does size matter? For me, firm size has not mattered, and does not. One size does not fit all. So, size up your situation. Be honest with yourself. Are you where you should be? Can you make it better? (Yes!) Remember, you have a license to practice law. If everything turns to dust tomorrow and your comfortable world collapses, you can still hang a shingle and earn a living as a lawyer from your kitchen. Knowing and believing that will let you focus on the only size issue that really causes us anxiety: it's almost summer and time to buy a new swimsuit.

Chapter 9:
Using personal interests to help make it rain

By Audra A. Dial, managing partner, Atlanta office of Kilpatrick Townsend & Stockton

When I started at the firm as a baby lawyer, I had no idea what business development was or how to do it. There weren't many women partners to look to for guidance, and for the most part, I saw the male partners taking their clients to play golf or out for a night on the town. I wasn't sure that I would ever be able to become a rainmaker because those entertainment options were not at all appealing to me.

Initially, I gave some thought to learning how to play golf but it didn't really stick with me because a) I don't really like to play golf, b) I had enough going on without adding mastering golf to my list, and c) it seemed boring. As I began developing friendships with women in-house counsel with whom I worked on cases, or to whom I was introduced through other lawyer friends, I noticed that many of them did not play golf either. For the most part, these women were around my age and seemed to have the same interests.

It then occurred to me that perhaps I could forge my own path by entertaining my clients in ways that would align with my personal interests, rather than just adopting the techniques that my male colleagues used. Since then, I have developed my own way of developing client relationships and generating business. My thoughts on how to make rain using your personal interests and talents – rather than trying to be someone else – are below.

Social outings
I first dipped my toe in the client development water by inviting

my women clients to dinner with their significant others. This seemed like a no brainer because I know I have limited time to spend outside of work. When I have the chance to spend time with my husband, we like to spend time with other couples and get to know them. I figured that my clients would feel the same way. And, in fact, these dinners were easy to set up. My in-house counsel friends wanted to get to know me better but also struggled with the same conflict: there's not enough time in the day to do everything you want to do. So, bringing their significant others along was an easy way for them to make time to get to know me better and also spend time with their loved ones.

This technique of doing something I wanted to do and turning it into a client event has become my signature approach to client development. For example, I'm now the proud mother of a seven-year-old boy. When I have time on the weekends, I want to spend it with him. Many of my in-house counsel colleagues are also parents and want to spend time with their kids on the weekends. So, I invite them to playdates at local museums or the children's theater. They get time with their kids and we get the chance to connect. A win-win and, again, an easy way for them to make time to get to know me.

Vision boarding

Once I became comfortable with these one-on-one activities, I started branching out into larger events where I would host a small group of my women clients for an activity. This started, again, from my belief that women would enjoy getting to know other women who were facing the same challenges, and from the fact that bringing like-minded women together is something I very much enjoy doing.

I first created an annual January event called "vision boarding". My first vision boarding party had only six people in attendance and was very rudimentary. I had read an article about how a vision board can help you focus on your goals more specifically, which interested me, and I figured my female peers would also be interested in focusing on their goals. That evening, we sat around with magazines, scissors, and glue sticks and created boards for our vision for the new year. We also spent time talking with each other about our specific goals and plans which enabled us to connect with each other more personally and learn how we could help each other achieve our goals for the year. (It was less about the boards and more about the bonding/connections.) Now, five years later, about 50 women attend my vision boarding party, and it's become quite popular. In fact, I'm often asked by women who have attended if they can bring their friends along and every year we have new people added to the group.

It is incredibly rewarding to be able to support my women clients with this fun event, and it gives me a perfect excuse to think more specifically about my own goals for the year. It also helps me solidify my role as a connector – helping women in-house counsel to build their networks of connections to other in-house counsel. I keep my vision boards in my office and use them as a personal reminder of what I want to accomplish each year. It's an effective way to not lose sight of your goals throughout the year and to stay connected to the women who are a part of the vision boarding experience.

Book club

After hosting the vision boarding event, I became a little bolder about creating gatherings that might be valuable experiences for small groups of women, and I started a book club for women in-house counsel. We meet once a year in the fall and discuss a book that I have selected and sent to the women in the spring. Our book selections have included *Lean In*, *The Confidence Code*, *Stiletto Network*, and last year's selection, *Year of Yes* by Shonda Rimes. The book club provides a platform for us to discuss how the book can help us achieve our goals and become better leaders, working women, and friends. And it's always interesting to hear what each woman takes away from the book. I have learned so much about my in-house counsel friends as a result of these discussions, and those lessons give me the opportunity to help my friends achieve their goals throughout the year.

Gift giving

In addition to hosting events, I also send my clients a gift to thank them for their business. As I thought about when to do this, I decided that the end of the year is a time when clients receive many gifts, and I would not be able to distinguish myself if I also sent a gift at that time. That prompted me to consider other holidays and times of the year, and I decided that daylight savings time, in March, was a unique time to send my thank-you gifts. Cookie Creations in Atlanta makes cookies in the shape of a sun, and I send these delicious sugar cookies out with a note about springing forward and enjoying the extra hour of sunlight to my key clients. These cookies are quite popular and appreciated equally by men and women. Doing this allows me to stay relevant and top-of-mind, thank my clients with a small token of my appreciation, and market to men and women without having to distinguish myself among the holiday gift-giving masses.

One more important point about the gifts I send to my clients – whether it is the book club book or the cookie. I don't send it in a plain old envelope. Instead, I use something that will get noticed: a red metallic envelope. Not only is red my favorite color, it signifies strength, power, and determination. Think about not just the gift itself, but also the timing and the packaging – it all matters. Find the right gift, timing, and packaging that defines your personal brand and use it as a way to distinguish what you're sending. When you get a red envelope from me, you know the item inside is special and not your typical work mail. Now the red metallic envelopes are my signature so when people see them peeking out of their inboxes, they get excited about what's inside.

Celebrating anniversaries of success

Another thing I like to do for my clients is to remind them of a success we've had together. Whether it is the anniversary of a substantial jury verdict we obtained or the date when we successfully negotiated a major settlement, I mark those dates with a recurring calendar entry that reminds me every year to check in with that client and congratulate them on our mutual success. It's a quick and easy way to reconnect with clients and remind them of one of the greatest results we've achieved together, not to mention it makes them feel good remembering that result. It's a small touch that lets my clients know I'm thinking about them, and it doesn't require much effort to do. Even when I'm pressed for time, I know I can send a quick email.

Monster jam

Although the activities and gifts I've described so far could all be considered highbrow, there are other times where clients appreciate doing something different and more colorful. One such activity is the monster truck rally known as Monster Jam. It's an event where monster trucks battle each other and smash each other's cars while the crowd cheers. They typically include lots of revving engines and rock music. Before I was a mom of a little boy, I never considered attending one of these events, but when my son was old enough to pay attention to TV, his eyes lit up when he saw the ad and asked if we could go. When we were there, I realized that the crowd was filled with moms and sons, and I hatched a plan for a client development event – a suite at the next year's Monster Jam. When I brought up this idea to others at the firm, the idea caught on fast and the suite was filled easily. Our clients loved the invitation, especially because they would not necessarily have been as adventurous as me when it came to bringing their children on their own. Also, this provided them the benefit of a suite to get away from the truck action while also allowing them the chance to spend time with their kids.

Holiday lights at the Botanical Garden

After creating this unique client event, I created a larger, office wide client event that has become the most popular and successful event for our office. It is a holiday event at the Atlanta Botanical Garden, where clients can bring their families and see the Garden lit up with holiday lights. The Atlanta Botanical Garden is a 30-acre garden located in the heart of our city, about a mile from our office, and every holiday season they cover the area with millions of lights and large-scale displays. It is quite the sight, and even more magical when viewing it with your awe-struck children, making it a perfect atmosphere for a family event. Throw in a face-painter for the kids, lots of delicious food, and a fully-stocked bar, and you've got yourself a "sell-out" event. It's hard to believe that our clients make time to come to this event when the holidays are so busy, but the event is so popular because they can include their families in the event.

Final thoughts

All of these events and activities that I created have stemmed from my personal interests. I enjoy spending time with my family so I try to create events where clients can do that too. I enjoy reading books about interesting women, and I figure my clients would like that too. I love being able to take in a fun concert or show, and I know my clients would want to do the same.

Strangely enough, I've even become a bit of a golf lover. Being in Atlanta, we are lucky enough to have tickets to the Masters tournament in nearby Augusta and although I have no desire to play golf, I don't mind watching it, especially on a beautiful spring day. And, I realized that most of my female clients aren't getting invited to the Masters because the men assume they wouldn't want to go, so they very much appreciate an invitation. Because I'm with them all day, it gives me the chance to really get to know my clients more deeply too.

When I was in law school, I never thought that much about how clients were developed or how I would ultimately be a successful rainmaker or be able to be a leader in the firm. I figured that successful rainmakers just got business because they did good work and clients kept coming back to them. I've since learned that it takes a lot more than good legal work to develop and retain clients. And, client development takes a lot of time and energy. It's really all about getting to know other people and leveraging your network to help your clients. In addition, it's about knowing yourself and being authentic.